THE RETURN OF THE CANE

Alder
(Alnus glu●

GERARD J. VAN DEN BROEK

# The Return of the Cane

*a Natural History of the Walking Stick*

. . . . . . .

*Illustrations Bas Mazur*

INTERNATIONAL BOOKS

ISBN 978 90 5727 050 5

© Gerard J. van den Broek, 2007

Design: Karel Oosting (koosting@mac.com)
Printing: A-D druk BV
Photo cover: Martin Hogeboom (www.mhfoto.nl)
Cover illustration: Bas Mazur
Photo author: Zwiebelfisch/Paul Kusters (www.
zwiebelfisch.nl)

Illustrations: Bas Mazur (www.basmazur.nl):
p. 2, 12, 18, 26/27, 31, 32/33, 36/37, 38, 40, 52/53,
61l+r, 67l+r, 68, 73, 76/77, 78, 81, 97, 98.
Photo's cane collection: Tony Fedeli (from:
Alfredo Lamberti, Bastoni da passeggio, 1994)
Photo's: Bettmann/Corbis: p. 11, 21, 46; Corbis:
p. 8, 25, 84/85, 107; Corbis/Sygma: p. 88/89;
Hulton-Deutsch Collection/Corbis: p. 22l+r;
Zuma/Corbis: p. 92; Rijksmuseum: p. 48.

English editing: Theodore J. van Houten
Production: Zwiebelfisch/Paul Kusters
(www.zwiebelfisch.nl)
Many thanks to: Jan Henk Berendsen,
Markelo (goastok)

Published by International Books
Grifthoek 151, 3514 JK Utrecht, the Netherlands,
phone (+31) 30 2731 840, fax (+31) 30 2733 614
i-books@antenna.nl, www.antenna.nl/i-books

# *Introduction*

. . . . . .

Over the years I have come to appreciate the company of my walking stick — it is actually more like a short staff — as an aid, as a means of defence against dogs, and even as an improvised monopod when taking photographs.

I cut it from a hazel bush some twenty-five years ago near a small brook in France, the Soudoire, running through the Département Corrèze. I used it on several holidays. But after a number of years it was left neglected for at least a decade. When I discovered it again I noticed that the peeled stick was still as fresh as if it had been cut only recently. On holiday in the Teutoburgerwald, Germany, I saw that these straight hazel walking sticks were very popular there. One could even buy steel tips in almost every shop to give a self-made stick that little extra. I added exactly such a tip to my French hazel stick, drilled a hole for a leather strap, and it had become a real staff! Later I even added a couple of tourist pilgrim insignia, which have an historical background which is also dealt with in this book.

Led by an interest in material culture as an entrance to man's cognition,[1] I decided to try and discover the roots of the stick and the staff in European history. I was struck by the huge range of sticks, staffs, crosiers and wands, each having its own cultural significance and practical or symbolic use. Of course, much more could be told about the staff in African and Asian cultures, and although I

decided to limit the scope of this essay to greater Europe, I am sure that many of the notions are also applicable to other ethnological fields of study.

I would like to point out that the inherent power of various kinds of trees must have been felt through the ages, and that it has gradually become the model on which to build a multitude of variations of power for ourselves.

## The Sphinx's Enigma

. . . . . .

It was at Thebes that the Sphinx's enigma was solved. Oedipus knew the secret of the riddle that no one had yet solved: *"What has one voice and becomes four-footed, two-footed, and three-footed?"* Oedipus answered: *"Man, crawling as a baby, then walking on two legs, and finally needing a cane in old age."* The Sphinx killed herself because Oedipus had solved the enigma. Oedipus was rewarded with the crown of Thebes [2] and married to Jocasta, the widowed queen.

The cane or staff, as in Sophocles' play, accompanying man in the last phase of life, is in its various forms a multi-faceted sign vehicle. It may indicate the lack of mobility of an elderly person while it also symbolizes royal omnipotence. Moreover, it is the symbol of healthy present day mountain hikers.

In today's stores and catalogues of outdoor equipment one finds devices of which the traditional forms could be seen mostly in the hands of old or at least sedate people, appearing in photographs taken around the turn of the nineteenth and twentieth centuries. It was the mountain hiking companion of both men and women: the cane or walking stick. It is evident that it is no longer the straight wooden branch of an ash, hickory, oak, hazel, or any other kind of deciduous tree. On the contrary, it has become high tech equipment made of aluminium alloy or even carbon fibre. It is telescopic, has an anti-slip end, and an ergonomic handle. Many types can even be fitted to a camera once the grip has been removed.

However, the cane has proven to be more than just the companion ensuring a solid grip on slippery or stony soil that it has been for many centuries. One even claims that it decreases the weight supported by the legs and feet as the arms take their share of the load, especially when backpacking. In short, it is a must for modern outdoor people. Recently, 'Nordic walking' has become popular. It is originally a summer time training method for cross-country skiing in Finland. Two sticks are used, thus exercising the entire body, and gaining speed while walking.

This dry-skiing training method is rapidly developing into a full-fledged sport. It even seems to challenge the popularity of traditional winter time sports. Especially middle-aged men and women seem to be attracted to it. It is promoted by tourist organisations and special Nordic walking training courses are given all over Western Europe. As is the case with Langlauf or cross-country skiing, special

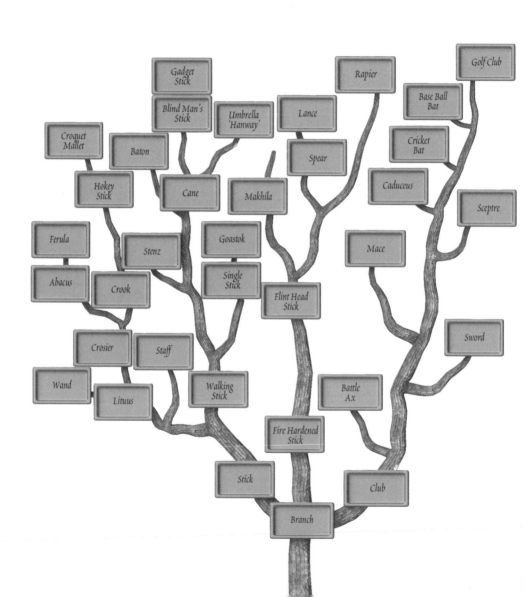

routes are planned in various kinds of terrain. Fortunately one usually sticks to the existing trodden paths. Thus a dangerous intrusion of pristine forests and valleys, so threatened by millions who take to the Alps each winter, is avoided.

## Genealogy of the Walking Stick

· · · · · ·

Man's rigid companion has many forms and attributions. Let us first have a look at the iconic variations of the archetypal stick or cane. There is the rod, staff, baton, crook, stave, walking stick, wand, sceptre, abacus, crosier, caduceus, mace, and so on. Each representation has its own domain or even owner: a shepherds crook, a pedestrian's walking stick, a conductor's baton, a herald's caduceus, Asclepius's or Aesculapius's rod, an officer's staff, a magician's wand, a king's sceptre, an emperor's mace, an abbot's crosier, a Knight Templar's abacus. Though the reconstruction of the genealogy of the present day walking stick is hazardous at least, a schematic representation gives us an insight into the family ties of its various phenotypes.

It obviously all started with a branch that fell off a tree. An *objet trouvé*, like the pebbles and stones that provided early hominids with their first tools and weapons.

From this first branch, a broad and lofty genealogical tree has emerged. The position from the tree's roots is an indication of the evolutionary stage. The vertical position in this system tells us the degree of kinship of the various members to one another. We are clearly talking about a candelabra model, in which the origin is formed by the archetypical 'branch'. Some family members stick out in this genealogy. They sprung rather early from their mutual origin. These family members are, perhaps not coincidentally mostly ceremonial objects with a highly symbolic rather than practical or functional value. They are the abacus, crosier and ferula on the left hand side, and the caduceus and sceptre on the right. The scheme of the stixonomy has to be bent round, as it were, in order to obtain the rapprochement of the two families, the 'Sticks' and the 'Clubs'.

In the middle we find two genera of sticks: the implements and weapons. Among them a number of rare species such as the Basque makhila, as a descendant of both.

## A Primeval Tool

. . . . . .

As a hunter and gatherer man has used the stick as a natural implement for many hundreds of thousands of years. This ubiquitous tool was used for digging, turning stones and poking in holes to search and find nutritious roots, insects, larvae and other small animals. Abundant in every forest and even on the savannah, the stick proved to be an excellent tool to accompany man on his daily routes, and seasonal trekking. Eventually, prehistoric man used fire to sharpen and harden its tip.

In the woods of a beautiful, narrow and forested cleft in the hills of the eastern part of the Luxemburg Ardennes, near Beaufort village and castle, a number of huge rocks emerge from the ground on which our ancestors sharpened their sticks and flints for thousands of years.[3] Deep tracks suggest that the surrounding area has been inhabited for a long period of time, and also that early man returned to this place frequently, to sharpen his essential companion, before gathering food. Unfortunately, it is not known what type of tree provided our ancestors with this material. The deep tracks, however, doubtlessly want us to assume that they used pine or deciduous wood, oak, ash or juniper, and other Northern hardwood trees.

The sharpened and hardened pointed stick would soon be used as a weapon as well, even before any kind of metal was applied. The development of the technique of splitting pebbles (Olduvai) into almost mass production of razor sharp blades was named after the Solutré culture in France. It influenced the evolution of the stick as a weapon. Lance and spear emerged from it. However, as soon as the stick turned into this kind of weapon, its multi-functionality disappeared. Because a stick with an accessory, such as a finely tailored flint stone blade or a precious bronze or iron head, was far too valuable to use for digging up roots or poking into holes to catch small game. Therefore, such a precious 'stick' was probably no longer carried with its head downwards, but upwards. Thus sparing its valuable assets and demonstrating that it had now become a weapon used against both man and beast. As a result, it now differed significantly from a pointed stick such as the common cane used for walking in the mountains. Though this walking stick is pointed too, its dangerous tip is pointing at the ground. Its steel tip is meant to give support and grip on steep or slippery soil. Though it is not intended as a weapon, skilled users can still defend themselves successfully with an ordinary walking stick. We will come to this later.

Our stixonomy shows us a very early family member of the branch, the club. A club is a relatively short, tapering piece of wood wielded mostly as a weapon, either functional or symbolic. Though seemingly irrelevant at the level of 'branch', the distinction between the stick and the club proved to be significant. It led to two different families sharing some characteristics, but 'converging' at the right and left extremes.

When we look at the genealogical tree, we are able to differentiate between five broad fields, distinguishing the quotidian implemental, the martial, the

magical, the (profane and liturgical) ceremonial, and the recreational. Within
the recreational domain we find 'playful' counterparts of originally 'serious' clubs
or sticks, just as we find the purely ceremonial versions of some deadly serious
martial equipment. We will also notice that liturgical and magic wands and staffs
are related.

In the field of the implemental we find the walking stick, the cane, and the
*cannes système* (gadget sticks), and also the umbrella. In the field of the martial
stick we see the headed and (fire-) hardened stick, the flint-headed stick that
evolved into the spear, and the longer variety, the lance with either a stone or
metal blade. Here we also find the sword and the rapier. They were entirely made
of metal, contrary to most other descendants of the 'stick'. There is, however, a
unique descendant of both the martial and the implemental stick. The makhila,
a most intriguing class in itself, was only made and used in the Basque area in the
South-West of France and the North-West of Spain.

Among the sticks of a magic nature, we find the wand and the lituus, both also
related to the (liturgical) staff.

Sticks of a ceremonial or liturgical character are: the staff, crook, crosier,
abacus and ferula. Their ceremonial, secular counterparts are the caduceus, the
mace, and the sceptre, descending from the club rather than from the stick. Their
symbolic value is comparable.

## The Universal Stick

. . . . . . .

The ordinary walking stick or cane is usually straight. It may end in a curved handle, and still comes in many shapes, and types. A farmer's stick was obviously no item of fashion. On the contrary, it was a device to help him walking the fields and slopes of the countryside, and to defend him against snakes, stray dogs, and even wolves in the old days. Even today, taking his herd to the field every morning and bringing it home in the evening, no French farmer would leave the village grounds without his habitual stick. Vivid tales are told of how this wooden companion had rescued him from venomous snakes flinging their fangs.

Various kinds of wood were used to make walking sticks, and the canes themselves often differed per region. Sometimes even their names vary. In the Massif Central (France) a stick obtained from the nut tree is called *boulade* instead of *canne*, referring to the boule — the thick, round part of the stick where root and stem meet, also found on German and English hazel walking sticks. Sometimes these rural canes were decorated by cutting images of lizards, frogs, and, much more rarely, anthropomorphic figures in the stick (cf. www.cannes-fayet.com). Obviously such types of sticks were not manufactured in large numbers, but cut by the owner himself.

Thouhg the rural stick may have been crudely decorated, imagination had no limits when it came to embelleshing manufactured luxurious walking sticks. This can clearly be seen as an expression of social status, and sometimes even as a way to transmit hidden messages. Frequently, the knobs or handles hid erotic symbols or representations. There were also numerous types of sticks that supported all kinds of devices, ranging from a compass to a small flask holding a few sips of spiritual liquid. People have always been extremely creative when it came to inventing built-in accessories for the walking stick. Remarkably enough, this type of stick is still being sold in Britain, where the large majority of the world's walking sticks are being made (cf. www.sticks.org/developmentandhistory2.htm, 2000). Through time, every social group proved to have its own type of walking stick, often quickly evolving into gadget-sticks. The seventeenth, eighteenth and nineteenth centuries show us an abundance of multi-functional walking sticks. Almost everyone could choose his own specific type. There were sticks for veterinarians and foresters, cattle salesmen (thin bamboo canes are still used on cattle markets in The Netherlands) and wine merchants, each with some kind of small implement to aid its owner in his profession, ranging from tasting wine to taking grain samples. Bird watchers would use a walking stick-telescope. A walking stick with a compass would not only very well suit the hiker, but the sailor as well. Albeit that walking sticks are rarely seen at sea, and only when one really needs one for lack of sea legs.

Thomas Hobbes (1588-1679) never left home without his cane. Its handle hid a pen and cow horn inkwell enabling him to immediately write down any thought that crossed his mind in a small notebook, stuck in his pocket (Van Os, 2001). Towards the end of his life Jean-Jacques Rousseau used a cane on his botanical hiking tours, when he wrote his 'Lettres élémentaires sur la botanique' (1771-1773). He was quite content with his walking stick, a gift from the Prince of Conti. Rousseau's stick was equipped with a very small spade to dig out plants growing out of reach from the forest paths. Moreover, the stick had a built-in magnifying glass to better determine the collected species. This was, incidentally, a heavily disputed approach of nature, as it was considered unnatural by most leading French botanists, such as Jussieu (cf. Van den Broek, 1986).

There were even fashionable canes for ladies in the eighteenth century,[4] though women were careful not to use a large one, in order to avoid the risk of being considered hindered in their go about town.

Walking stick culture reached its peak in nineteenth century Europe. The cane often functioned as an emblem of one's social class, not just of one's profession or hobby. In England and France every profession had its own type of cane. Frequently, different sticks were used at different times of the day. There were actually canes for morning, afternoon, tea and evening use! In the city there were typical strolling canes or *boulevardeurs*. These were meant as a focal point of attention for the passers-by, and they acted as a sign of wealth if they were made of expensive materials. Obviously, the cane used by a farmer at the weekly cattle market distinguished itself from the stick in the hands of a London City solicitor. The first was most probably home-made and came from the hedges surrounding the farmer's fields. The latter was possibly purchased in Bond Street, delicately carved and made of selected, exotic wood. It would have had a handle featuring a gun dog, a species of fowl, or a luscious female. Canes were a fashion accessory not only in England, but in early nineteenth century France as well. Dozens of different types could be found in the various walking stick catalogues of the day (cf. www.cannes-fayet.com).

The oldest and most common gadget stick is of course the umbrella. There is evidence that it was known already in ancient Egypt, Assyria, Greece, and China. It was initially designed for protection against the sun (umbra is Latin for shadow). The Greek and Chinese were the first to wax or lacquer their umbrellas to protect themselves against the rain as well. It was not until the sixteenth century, however, that the *brollie* became popular in Europe, and first seen as an accessory only suitable for women. Jonas Hanway (1712-1786), a Persian writer, carried and used it in public in England for over thirty years, thus making it popular among men, too. In England, where the first all-umbrella shop — James Smith and Sons, Hazelwood (!) House [5] — was opened in 1830 in London, an umbrella is sometimes still called a 'hanway' (cf. Bellis, 2004; Atkin, 2004).

*Walt Whit*
*Kenney, 18*
*Boston, Ma*
*setts, USA*

Straight walking sticks made before 1819 were made out of a single piece of wood. When curved they consisted of two parts: the stick and the handle. It was Michael Thonet (1798-1871), the German furniture designer, who invented the art of bending straight branches of beech (*Fagus sylvatica*) and oak (*Quercus*, var. species) by steaming the sticks under very high temperatures. This makes it quite easy for the collector to date a walking stick, since from 1819 onwards, Michael Thonet produced his own designs built from bentwood (Bugholz) in Boppard am Rhein.[6] This seemingly simple invention gave a boost to the manufacture of walking sticks, as from that moment it was possible to give the walking stick a curved handle, which led to the production of millions of such sticks.

# Cannes de conscrits

. . . . . . .

The most peculiar walking sticks, however, were found in France. The so-called *cannes de conscrits* (canes of conscripts) were made of glass. They were the symbol of young men called up for military service in the eighteenth century. At that time the French general Jourdan launched the very unpopular conscription in order to provide the armies of the Directoire with cannon fodder, as voluntary service apparently did not provide enough. Being called up for military service implied a real initiation rite for young adult men in France. It was a sign of virility which occurred when these young men were of marital age. On various occa-

*conscrit*

sions, the 'conscrits' pinned *cocardes* on their jackets, saying: 'Bon pour les filles' (up for girls). The day they were registered and had their medical check-up, the soldiers-to-be danced in the streets of their home town. They sang and drank in the cafes and visited the brothels, canes in hand. Frequently, these canes were made of coloured or transparent glass, and filled with candy or liquor.

There were also wooden canes decorated with nails and painted spirals in red, white and blue (the colours of the French 'tricolore' flag), and adorned with colourful ribbons. There was a certain likeness with the sticks used by the majorette troupe leaders accompanying local show bands in present day street parades. The real canne de conscrit, however, was made of blown, hollow red, white, and blue striped glass, and had a round knob. It was filled with the wine or liquor the conscripts drank in the local pubs where they gathered before, and after their duty service (cf. Segas, 2002). While its owner was in service, or even in battle, the canne and its content waited for him to come home safely. The ritual clearly had the character of a magic spell about it: leaving a bit of spirit behind meant it would be collected later on.

These glass canes very much resembled the coloured and striped candy walking sticks with their curved handle, seen at Christmas in sweet shops, and the straight striped 'Brighton Rock' candy sticks sold at fun fairs in Europe. One may clearly see them as the 'offspring' of the cannes de conscrits that are no longer used.

# The Stenz

. . . . . . .

In Europe we see that the more special types of sticks were particularly found among men, and especially young men. In France and Germany, but in other European countries as well, the tradition of young men learning a craft, roaming their country from one apprenticeship to another to improve their skills and make some money, remained vivid for centuries. In France not only young craftsmen travelled from town to town. Until recently young peasant's sons also tried to earn their bread by finding a farmer who would actually pay them for their work, something their father usually could not afford. If a young farmer wanted to get married he had to do his 'tour' first to earn money. These young men, peasants and craftsmen alike, were called 'les compagnons du tour de France' (cf. Barret & Gurgand, 1974). The German counterparts of the 'compagnons', the 'Wandergesellen' from the 'Gesellenzünfte' (guilds) were 'auf die Walz.' This ancient tradition was found particularly among young blacksmiths, masons and carpenters.

Remarkably enough, these young men were dressed and equipped almost identically, at least in Germany. They wore a large black brimmed hat, a white shirt, a black coat, a sac with a shoulder strap, and carried a letter of introduction to any future employer, and their 'Stenz', a stout, twisted stick. They roamed about, and were not allowed to come within a radius of 50 kilometres of their home town. The Wandergesellen were not even supposed to stay in one place longer than three months as to remain 'strangers'. They were not allowed to pay for their meals or for a place to sleep. They lived from the gifts of villagers such as the minister, the chaplain, or other notables. Their place to sleep was a barn or a shed. Such apprentices needed to have a faultless past, and they had to live perfectly immaculate lives (cf. Barret & Gurgand, 1974; www.confédération compagnonnages européen.fr; www. rechtschaffene-zimmerer.de; www.gemeinde-gersdorf.de).

Their tour was obviously very much that of a pilgrim. Even their outfit looked quite similar. The phenomenon may be seen as a secular counterpart to the long pilgrimages to Santiago de Compostela, dating back to at least the thirteenth century. It is remarkable that an enthusiastic revival of the 'Walz' can be observed to have taken place over the last twenty odd years.

## *The Goastok*

. . . . . . .

In the Netherlands the same system of apprenticeship for craftsmen was known in the Middle Ages. The journeymen must also have had their own sticks. A very typical walking stick is the 'goastok' (linguistically akin to the German Gehstock, walking stick) from Markelo, a traditional village in the Twente region. This

*Blackthorn*
*(Prunus spir*

unique type of stick recently experienced a revival after it had disappeared for decades. It has always been made out of medlar or blackthorn (*Prunus spinosa*). The Goastok is adorned with a very remarkable handle. It is woven in a black and white chequered pattern out of split quills of geese and hair of jet black, preferably Frisian horses. The handle is adjusted with small round-headed brass nails around its top, crowned by an oversized nailed cap similar to those used to smoothly slide a chair over a carpet. The goastok was a natural companion for men at a time when walking was still the usual way to move about in this area. It acted as a walking stick, and also as a serious weapon of defence against dogs and the highway men, threatening travellers in the countryside until the second half of the nine-

*Goastok*

teenth century. Farmers, hawkers and cattle traders alike brandished their goastok. Young men wanting to look smart when they went out courting also carried their stick, sometimes to settle a quarrel over a girl.

Besides its practical function, the goastok served a ceremonial purpose. When a wedding was due young men would knock their sticks on the doors of the couple's friends and family to invite them to the wedding (cf. Egberts, 2005; Boxma, 2001).

Taking a closer look at the materials chosen to make this particular stick, it appears that the same type of wood was used as for the makhila. Perhaps even more significant, however, are the goose quills and horse hair used for the handle.

Goose feathers are basic material for a number of artefacts. They are used to fledge arrows, and the goose also provided the superior writing instrument for many centuries. Hundreds of thousands of quills were dipped in ink from the early Middle Ages until the nineteenth century. Quills of geese are still used to make badminton shuttles, for instance. Smaller feathers fill the lining of downs, pillows and mattresses. Traditionally, goose feathers were collected by gypsies, throughout Europe.

Horse hair also has a multitude of applications in the arts and crafts. It is used manufacturing military uniforms and hats. Fine brushes and bristles are made out of horse hair as well, and it is still used in bedding and cricket balls. Until the nineteenth century, it was used for tying (fly-)fishing lines. It is the essential material used to make bows for string instruments. Moreover, whips and the like were also made of horse hair.

It is noteworthy that horses were the traditional 'merchandise' of gypsies for many centuries in Europe. String instruments are traditionally associated with these people. Consequently we may state that connecting goose quills and horse hair was the gypsy's doing. Why would that have any significance for the goastok in Twente? The answer lies in the rather unpleasant history of this lovely country district. In the eighteenth century strangers, deserted soldiers, Jews, tramps and gypsies in particular were fiercely prosecuted by both civilians and militia men. Even lynch parties were not uncommon in Twente in those days (cf. Schlüter, 1994).

The goastok also had a function as a life preserver, and it was hung above the conjugal bed after the wedding ceremony. It was a symbol of virility and surely used as a weapon against the outcasts of society, the despicable ones, the heathens who deserved punishment. And it is exactly this story that the handle of the goastok tells us. It is a sign of preemptive victory over these characters, symbolised by goose quills and horse hair in the hands of the prosecutor. Both materials stand for the means of subsistence of the Roma, who in turn act as metonymy for all people who were not quite voluntarily on the move.

Eventually the goastok almost disappeared when bicycles became so popular that walking from one village to another became an exception, the locals say.

## The Makhila

. . . . . . .

Halfway between a fierce weapon and a walking stick or staff is the Basque makhila, a most interesting and mysterious device with a very long history. At first glance the makhila looks like a straight, characteristic walking stick with a blunt clover-like bottom end for a firm grip on rocky or slippery soils. The upper end, however, is much more interesting. For, here its secret is hidden in a metal manchete and a flattened ball: a 12 cm razor-sharp blade, hand-forged out of high quality steel. This can turn the makhila from a stick into a spear. Moreover, the hollow ball is half filled with lead. It is therefore a dangerous multi-functional weapon: stick, dagger or spear. Thanks to the tough wood of the medlar (*Mespilus germanica*, 'mizpirondoa' in Basque) is is also very solid. Again we see the significance of turning a stick upside down: the function of a cane alters completely. When held at the other end it becomes very dangerous. In order to be effective, a makhila is perfectly made to measure. Length, weight and strength of its future owner are just as important as the chosen materials itself. As a result no two makhilas are alike. In the mountainous Basque area, the makhila can be found in every home, in every lodge in the woods, in every shepherd's cabin. Even when

*Makhila*

deserted in winter, for no one would as much as even dream of stealing a makhila. A makhila is never purchased, it can only be a gift.

Making a makhila is a wonderful and secretive process. The first phase is the search for a suitable branch of around three metres length with a fine grain and high density, supple yet strong: it must be virtually unbreakable. The next step involves making cuts in the bark, 'le marquage,' with a special knife. This takes place in spring when the juices of the live tree flow fully. These incisions vary from snake-like figures to 'pointillism'. Later, these cuts and dents become scars in the wood itself. In late autumn, when the juice has stopped flowing, the sticks are harvested. The makers of makhilas keep it a secret where they work the medlar tree.

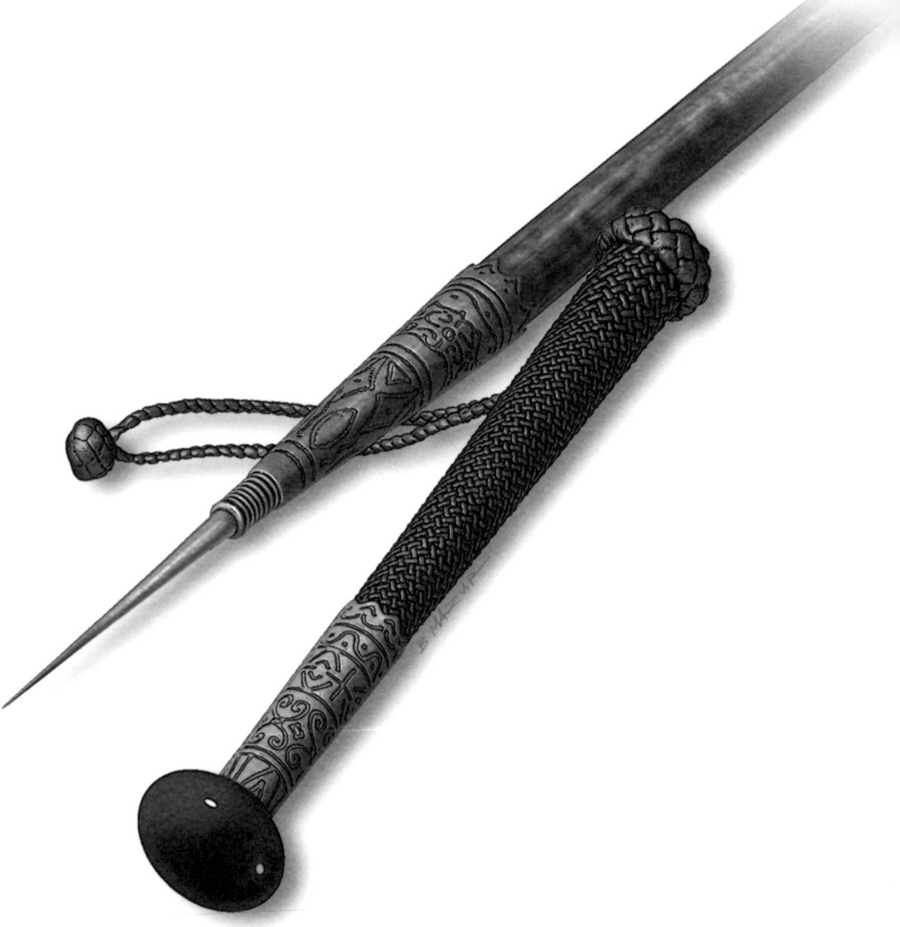

After a lengthy drying process in an oven, the wood is dyed to give it its patina. Its parts are precisely fitted together to obtain the right balance for using it both as a walking stick, and as a weapon. The ferrules are made of brass. The ball hiding the dagger may be made out of African cow horn, copper or brass, gold or even crystal. Such precious materials are mostly reserved for makhilas offered as a gift to world-renowned personalities, such us a head of state, the Pope, a famous sportsman or scientist. The brass balls are engraved for embellishment, but also to give it a better grip. Moreover, most makhilas are personalised by engraving the name of its owner in Basque.

Makhilas are said to have played an important part in the history of pilgrimage. It is remarkable that rather makhila-like staffs can often be found in (late) mediaeval drawings and etchings of pilgrims and saints on pilgrimage. Most probably, these staffs actually were makhilas. Pilgrims were not allowed to carry weapons on their sacred route of repentance. Sinners's ingenuity, however, solved this problem by 'inventing' the makhila with its hidden dagger. The church knew very well that pilgrimage was not without danger. The blessing pilgrims received alluded to the staff as a support for their journey, enabling them to defeat the throngs of enemies doubtlessly to be met on their journey.

Remarkably each of the three sole centres in the world where makhilas are still made, lie on the route to Santiago de Compostela. In France, however, such a pil-

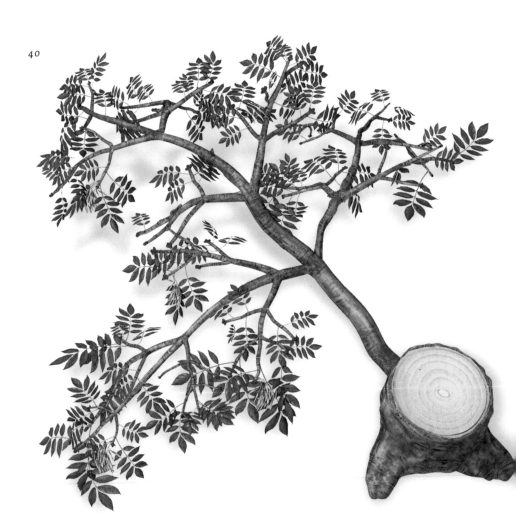

grim's stick was called a *bourdon*, and known as the pilgrim's fifth member. It was a stout stick, its length ranging up to the heart of the person carrying it. It was often decorated with religious scenes cut into the wood. At the upper end there was a ball, just like the makhila, or a sculpted ring around it. The lower part ended in a sharp metal tip (cf. Segas, 2002). Smugglers dragging their contraband across the Pyrenees may also have used the makhila or bourdon both as an aid, and as a weapon while crossing these still wild and uninhabited mountains.

## Duelling Sticks

. . . . . . .

Until the early 1920's the unarmed stick or singlestick was a weapon for those not allowed to wear rapiers or swords. Especially in Great Britain. The singlestick was also used in the serious sport of cudgelling.

'*The weapon is a good stout ash-stick with a large basket handle. The players are called gamesters [...] and their object is simply to break one another's heads: for the moment that blood runs an inch anywhere above the eyebrow, the old gamester to whom it belongs is beaten, and has to stop.*' (Hughes in: Amsberger, 1998).

Singlestick fighting was rather similar to another rural kind of duelling: 'bekkensnijden' (face cutting) in The Netherlands (cf. Van Lennep: 28-30). Both were a crude

form of the nobility's elegant yet deadly duels using rapiers. It is remarkable that in both types of fighting among commoners the combatants aimed at their opponent's head whereas in 'real' duelling every part of the body could be a target. It has been recorded that a singlestick combatant was arrested for hitting the other party on the inside of the knee, which was regarded as foul play (cf. Amsberger, 1998). This kind of stick-work was also practiced as a popular way of self-defence around 1900. An ordinary cane was seen as an effective weapon to stave off any attack by an adversary, whether armed with a cane or an alpenstock. Though to the layman stick fighting would seem quite similar to the graceful combat of two *épée* wielding noblemen, nothing could be further from the truth. Self-defence was definitely not a game. The walking stick was used as a life preserver, and aimed at the attacker's head, like in a single-stick fight. But the crook of a walking stick was also used to be either hooked on the assailant's neck or leg. Pearson's Magazine of February 11th, 1901, offers the advice that, once attacked, for instance, one should:

' [...] *make a slightly threatening motion with your left hand, as though you intended to seize the left hand of your assailant in order to belabour him with your stick. The object of this feint is only to engage your adversary's attention and make him look at your left hand whilst you suddenly dart your right arm forward, and hook him by the neck in the crook of your stick. Directly you have hooked him, bend your knees well so as to throw the whole weight of your body upon him, whilst you pull him with his face towards the ground.*'

1-Wright,
e with
-stick,
n's
, 11, 1901

Even a light cane was seen as an effective weapon when attacked by someone with a stout stick. It could be used against a skilled boxer or even against a crowd. This type of self-defence using a walking stick was even recommended as a most exhilarating and graceful exercise, according to the Pearson's Magazine article.

Farmers, too, used their walking sticks for self-defence. But they could also protect themselves with agricultural tools such as the flail for freshing wheat, barley, and oats. The flail consisted of a short stick or club, called a swizzle, hanging at a leather strap from a long wooden handle known as the staff. The swizzle struck the grain and flailed it from the heads. In various cultures the flail became an effective and more or less concealed peasant weapon, to be found on every farm. It proved an excellent alternative for the more professional weapons of soldiers and the nobility that farmers were often not allowed to possess. Despite this prohibition farmers obviously wanted to defend themselves effectively, and so they tried to find ways to do so. As a result, a fair number of oriental martial arts incorporate a variety of agricultural tools that made fierce weaponry in the hands of expert fighters.

*From:*
*E.W. Barton*
*Self-defence*
*a Walking*
*in: Pearson*
*Magazine*

. . . . . .

Sometimes seemingly common representations of material culture become famous. And this may happen at any time. It also applies to the cane. Four centuries ago the great playwright, poet, and writer from the Low Countries, Joost van den Vondel (1587-1679) wrote his tragedy 'Palamedes' (1625) about the public execution — beheading — of Johan van Oldenbarneveldt (1547-1619), a popular governor in the period known as the Dutch Golden Age. Vondel referred to the sound of the governor's cane on the sidewalks in the governmental centre at the Hague. Upset by the unfair trial against this elderly statesman, Vondel brought the reassuring sound of Van Oldenbarneveldt's cane, and his respected appearance successfully back to memory. Thus he severely criticized the executioners of this statesman, popular even with the common people. Vondel also wrote a famous satire featuring Oldenbarneveldt's stick right after the execution, 'Het Stockske'. It was not published until 1658.

Another much more widely known stick first appeared on the silver screen a few months before wwi: Charlie Chaplin's bamboo cane. His stardom, and with it the fame of his cane in cinema, began in 1914, when he first appeared as 'The Tramp' or 'The Little Fellow.' Looking undersized and undernourished, Chaplin wore a battered derby hat, a coat too small for him, and pants much too large. His

shuffling suggested he had never worn a pair of shoes his own size. Yet this City of London figure of poverty also wore gloves and carried a bamboo cane, seeming to reflect a spirit that bounces back from the most crushing defeats. The last shot in many of Chaplin's silent films shows him walking off into the distance. The Tramp was homeless and penniless once more. But with his hat tilted and swinging his cane he was ready again for whatever adventure lay around the corner. Chaplin's cane was often used as a prop, stopping revolving doors, etc. It was extensively used in various ways in the 1916 comedy short 'The Rink'.

## *Factual and Virtual Power*

. . . . . .

When looking at the stixonomy again, we see that the caduceus, the mace and the sceptre — without purely implemental functional values — have an obtained and ascribed symbolic significance, dating back as far as Egypt's pharonic dynasties. Though the heka, for instance, strongly resembles the crooked staff, it is usually much smaller, its dimensions equaling a common sceptre. This was the principal attribute of Osiris, and symbolised government and good behaviour of the people (cf. Lam, 2003). The so-called sceptre of the god Ouas was the symbol of power and domination, and may be described as an ordinary straight staff, even

though it has a forked lower end. It derived from the type of stick used for catching snakes. The ancient Egyptians had a variety of sticks and sceptres, each having their own name and purpose, though they are very hard to distinguish from one another (cf. Gardiner, 1976). They can still be found among the nomadic Peuls: the yat (also the name of the beautiful 'stick' used in the synagogue to point at verses in the Thora), lappata, mawndu, butturu, booldu, nafooru and hogatu. In both — formerly neighbouring — cultures, most of the words for stick, sceptre and staff allude to power, and to verbs as to rule, command, govern, and so on. The use of crooked staffs in particular was, and still is restricted to people with achieved or ascribed status, varying from the Pharaoh in ancient Egypt to members of the council of elders among the Peuls, the Dogon and Hogons of Mali (cf. also Lam, 2003).

In the Classical period, Hermes' or Mercury's caduceus, which has two snakes curled around it, is an offspring of the club, like the sceptre and the mace. Hermes, son of Zeus, delivered his messages with miraculous speed as he wore winged sandals (talaria), a broad-brimmed winged hat (petasus), and carried a winged staff. The Greeks called Hermes's staff kerykeion, 'messenger'. The Latin word for it was caduceus. In antiquity most messengers and travellers wore a hat similar to Hermes'/Mercury's petasus to protect them from the sun. This attribute is also found among the pilgrim's standard equipment. Ordinary, mortal messengers in the Classical period also carried a staff to identify themselves so they could travel freely. Hermes/Mercury later became associated with magic and science, but he also became the patron saint of shepherds (!), tradesmen and thieves (Hope Moncrieff: 12). The caduceus also represents the World Axis, at the same time separating and combining the good and the evil forces of the earth, which notion is probably of Egyptian origin. Hermes'/Mercury's caduceus is frequently confused with the originally single-snake crutch of Aesculapius, the Roman god of healing; thus symbolizing the healing power of this Deity and latter day physicians.

The mace differs from the caduceus mainly in its cultural significance. It is a club-shaped object used as a symbol of authority. It is most often seen in legislatures where it is mainly used to restore order. The mace was originally a mediaeval weapon. It was a long-handled club, heavily weighted at one end. As the science of war developed, the weighted end became an iron ball. Archers, mounted warriors and footmen used the mace as a hand arm. Sergeants at arms, who guarded kings and nobility, and some church officials, also carried maces. Gradually the mace gained a ceremonial character. The one used in the United States House of Representatives, for instance, is about three feet (90 centimetres) long, and consists of ebony rods bound with a silver band. A longer ebony rod at the centre of the bundle has a silver globe on it, and a silver eagle on top resembling the phalanx, a weapon already found in Biblical times.

Today's 'sergeant at arms' is an officer keeping order at the meetings of clubs and deliberative bodies, usually legislatures. He may serve the assembly in several ways, and has the power to compel members to attend sessions when their presence is needed to make a quorum. Each branch of the US Congress, for instance, has an office for a sergeant at arms. When the sergeant at arms carries the mace down the aisle of the legislature, all disorder must cease, and any disorderly member is found in contempt.

It is assumed that King Richard I of England — The Lion Hearted — created the office of sergeant at arms. Richard appointed a corps of twenty-four body-guards to attend, and guard him. It is even plausible that the US-sergeant's office stems from a tradition in the Middle Ages, when a saying stated: *'No land without a lord, and no lord without land.'* One could only become a vassal of the lord through a ceremony called 'homage'. During this initiation rite the future vassal promised to be loyal, defend the lord and his possessions, and become his man. The ceremony being reciprocal in character, implied that in turn the lord promised to treat the vassal with honour and dignity. After performing homage, the new vassal was invested with his fief. This was done in an investiture ceremony, at which the lord gave his vassal a clod of dirt, and a stick, symbolizing the fief (Biel, 1994).

The stick may be seen as a *pars pro toto* of the power of his lord. And indeed, a part for the whole it was: for the vassal received only the use or possession of the fief, not full ownership of it. He held the fief in return for services he had to render. As long as the vassal held the fief, he received what the land — and the peasants on it — produced. He collected taxes, held court, administered justice, and managed the peasants' labour. The vassal's power, however, depended on that of the lord, which was symbolized by the stick rendered to him when he received the fief. This implies a relationship between the land, and the stick. The fief was represented by the stick. Thus there existed an intricate relationship between the lord, the vassal, the fief and the stick. As we have seen, the fief was not a real gift, even though we realize that a strong connection existed and persisted between the giver, the fief,

*Mace*

and the receiver (cf. Biel, 1994; Mauss, 1925; Poly & Bournazel, 1990). This relation was based on reciprocity, the mutual exchange of priviliges.

A staff without political or religious significance, but with all the necessary attributed power, exclusively used at one type of occasion, can be found in (Dutch) universities. It is a tall staff with silver ornamentations, used by the Pedel — a university official — in a doctoral promotion ceremony. The Pedel interrupts the actual doctorate exam, that has has all the hallmarks of a lay ceremony, by tapping his staff, announcing "hora est" (time is up). That ends many a candidate's ordeal.

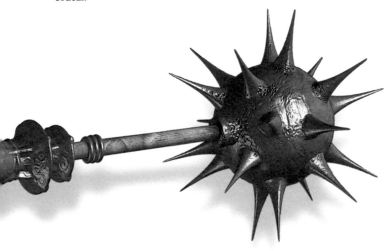

# Playful Sticks and Clubs

. . . . . . .

So definitely not all 'sticks' are or were merely used for support or self-defence. The French-Italian composer and music director Jean-Baptiste Lully (1632-1687) beat time with his usual staff. Unfortunately, one day he got angry at a rehearsal, and injured his foot while furiously beating time. Shortly afterwards he died of a gangrenous infection. Lully's type of staff is currently no longer in use. But there is the conductor's baton, a usually short, frail stick to enhance the gestures or stop the playing while rehearsing and conducting an orchestra.

Clearly then, in specific situations, people are able to command a crowd with a stick only slightly larger than a new pencil. Though indeed small, the baton is still a sign of authority demanding the attention of an orchestra. By wielding it, some hundred odd people may be ruled at a time. It is used to beat time, and to draw the attention of the players by tapping on the conductor's stand when the musicians have to stop playing or even talking. The conductor's baton is very much an authoritarian implement that rules out any form of discussion. In that particular way only it is similar to the sceptre, which is purely symbolical and no functional instrument. Perhaps less authoritative, but definitely drawing attention is the sport or recreational activity in which individuals twirl a baton, in the form of a thin metal rod. Baton twirlers perform and compete singly or in squads or teams. They combine intricate turns and tosses of the baton with dancing, and gymnastic movements. Skilled twirlers can simultaneously wirl and toss batons in both hands.

Most baton twirlers use rubber-tipped batons made of aluminium or other lightweight metal. Some twirlers use novelty batons with hoops, ribbons, fire, or pompons for show effects. Baton twirlers called majorettes or even cheerleaders perform alongside marching bands at sports events, and in street parades. Baton twirl competitions are held at all levels of competence.

Another type of baton is used by two competing teams of runners, the first of whom carries a baton of about a foot long (30 centimetres). After running a certain distance, called a leg, the athlete hands the baton over to the next team member. This exchange must occur within a zone twenty meters long. If the runners do not exchange the baton within this zone, their team is disqualified. Relays are run by teams of four runners.

The unifying element in these three examples where batons are used is clearly that the one who has the lead also carries the stick. Here too the baton literally stands for authority and leadership.

There are, however, more 'playful' sticks and clubs. The hockey stick and golf club are the oldest and best known ones. Although they differ in use, cultural domain and symbolic value from many other related equipment, both the hockey stick, and the golf club stem from the same origin: a branch fallen off a tree. Hockey has its 'stick' and golf its 'club'. Although they have the same forebear the hockey stick is said to be related to the shepherd's crook, 'hoquet' in French, but used the other way round. Both, however, are meant to slap an object and not to 'stick' something or give support. They both have a secondary type of use, and not a primary one, like most other sticks and clubs. This stems from the simple fact that they are meant to hit a ball. This ball has the primary function, as it should hit the target or disappear into a hole.

Their sign value is comparable. Like in most upper class sports the ball is not touched by hand, but only propelled by using an instrument. It thus generates some socio-cultural significance. Both hockey and golf are still associated with significantly higher socio-cultural and socio-economic layers of society than such direct contact sports as soccer. That is why carrying a hockey stick or showing off a golf caddy full of clubs — or better still, driving one — seems to tells us so much about their owner.

There is also the croquet mallet, crucial to playing this 'gentle but wicket game,' that originates from the mediaeval French *paille maille* (from Latin: palla mallens = ball and mallet) played by the plain inhabitants of the thirteenth century country side, wielding their mailles in such a way that the balls rolled through willow wood or iron hoops. The game was exported to England, where it became known as 'Pall Mall'. In France it gradually drifted into oblivion, to be reintroduced in the mid-nineteenth century, when it obtained its present form. It became popular in America at the same time. Here, too, it was a sport for the idle class, like golf, but not half as serious (cf. Reaske:14-19). The name of the game, 'croquet' seems to come from the French 'crochet,' 'croc' or 'croche', linking it directly to the shepherd's crook, obviously referring to the shape of the early mallets. In Ireland, the game was even called 'crooky' (Reaske: 25). It is remarkable that the character, function and cognitive connotation of a stick, i.e., the crook, is profoundly changed the moment it is held upside down, much like the pointed stick that was eventually provided with a separate flint stone, bronze or iron head. In this case an important implement and companion of shepherds and clergymen became an instrument of play just by holding the wrong end of the stick. When they were boys the present author and his brother did this too, using their grandfather's walking stick. As can be expected it was certainly not appreciated. Adults generally have a much more 'traditional' way of handling this type of material culture, because of the conventional cultural codes it represents. Children usually do not bother about them.

Although the name of the 'cricket' game is almost similar to 'croquet' it is a completely different sport. Even though it also involves a wicket that has to be targeted by a ball. Cricket, too, is an age-old game, though not as ancient as croquet. It was first mentioned in Britain in the first quarter of the seventeenth century. The cricket bat as we now know it however, would amaze the players from those days, as it evolved from a hockey stick-like club to the present broad, flat shape. So the origins of both games are also quite similar. In turn the baseball bat originated from the cricket bat during the first half of the nineteenth century. It represents a recent offspring of the club and stick family, initially found among the same leisure class we saw earlier.

## Reverential 'Sticks'

. . . . . .

One of the most important and extended families in the genealogy of the branch is the ceremonial stick, often used in liturgical settings. The staff and the crook are found in both the implemental and the ceremonial domain. However, the crosier, abacus and ferula are of a strictly ceremonial, even liturgical nature. Not only did the Roman Catholic bishop and the Greek and Russian orthodox clergies carry a staff or crosier ever since mediaeval times. The official and later liturgical staff, symbol of reverence and significance, is much older than that.

The Old Testament tells the story of the Jewish people's exodus from Egypt. Their flight was halted by the Red Sea. With his staff Moses 'divided' the waters 'and the children of Israel went into the midst of the sea upon the dry ground: and the waters were a wall unto them on their right hand, and on their left.' (Exodus XIV: 15-22). With 'a strong east wind all that night' the waters were divided, allowing the Jewish people to cross this barrier between Egypt and the Promised Land. The Egyptians persued, and went in after them to the midst of the sea (XIV: 23) and the Lord overthrew the Egyptians 'in the midst of the sea.' (XIV: 27). There remained 'not so much as one of them' (XIV: 28). Apparently, Moses had an ambiguous relation with sticks. He once fled for one, that suddenly turned into a snake. Exodus also tells the story of Aaron, who 'stretched out his hand with his rod, and smote the dust of the earth' and saw how 'the dust of the land became lice throughout all the land of Egypt.' (VIII: 16-17).

The staff not only played a special role in Judeo-Christian mythology. In ancient Greece, we find a staff that was crucial to Tiresias. While watching Pallas Athena bathing, he was struck with blindness when she splashed water in his eyes. Afterwards the goddess felt sorry for him. Although she did not restore his eyesight, she gave him a staff enabling him to walk safely. Tiresias eventually died when he drank from Tilphosa's well (Brewer: 1230). Nemesis, the goddess of Revenge, also carried a staff. It was made of ash, the tree that acted as one of her disguises (cf. Clarke Nuttall, 1916; Fraanje: 114).

There is an entire score of saints with a staff as typical attribute in the Christian pantheon and its iconology. During the first two centuries ad, the term 'saint' referred specifically to professores, confessores and martyrs. Through the Martyres Acts (*Acta Martyres*) true saints could be distinguished from false ones. Local people were only allowed to worship these saints after an official 'beatificatio'

*her*

*St. Dominic*

from the local bishop. Beatificatio could lead to canonization when neighbouring bishops implicitly or explicitly accepted the beatificatio.

In the early days of the adoration of martyrs, local worshippers gathered at martyrs' tombs on the anniversaries of their deaths. After the substantial extension of the list of saints with numerous martyrs, bishops, monks, scholars, miracle-workers, and other heroes or heroines, their relics were considered to give special blessings. People asked saints to plead with God for special favours. Particular practices developed around the veneration (*cultus duliae*) of many Christian saints, later often considered as superstition. Nevertheless, the names and sacred places of these would-be saints still exist today. Many such locations became places of pilgrimage, where staffs and sticks played an important role. They still do as a matter of fact, as we shall see later.

Through the centuries, saints were attributed with various paraphernalia to easily identify them in paintings, sculpture groups or statues. A 'true' iconic and recognizable image or statue was impossible in most cases. Therefore many saints are not the factual representation of a historical person. In fact, no exact description exists of most holy figures. We can understand the difficulty of the identification of saints if we consider the 'vera eikon' (true image) of Jesus Christ, and the Turin shroud. In short, a material object has always acted as a welcome indexical sign for the saint one would like to address. The spread of liturgical items developed with the elaboration of the worship service, beginning in the late ninth century. The expansion of the Roman Catholic liturgy led to the creation of many objects, vessels called pyxes, to hold Communion wafers, and reliquaries containing body parts of saints, or (fragments of ) crosiers or staffs.

In countless churches in Europe, statues of saints can be found holding a staff: Jesus' foster father, Joseph; St. Peter and St. Paul, St. Macarius, St. Bartholomew, St. Dominic, St. Tranus of Parada, St. Bruno, St. Adelbert, St. John Gualbeito, St. Christopher, St. Martialis, St. Anthony Abbot, St. Raymundus, St. Romuald, St. William of Maleval, St. Willibrord, St. Jude, St. James Minor, and of course St. James the Great, St. Fridolin, St. Judoc, St. Roch, St. Pirmin; the Saints from Arles sur Tech in France: St. Aydan and St. Asaph; St. Loy (or Eligius), patron saint of blacksmiths, holding a hammer as well; St. Philip and St. Domitian.

In such countries as France, Spain and Italy, probably even more holy figures can be found carrying a staff, not belonging to official clergy, but to the richly endowed popular pantheon. The ones mentioned here should be sufficient to wonder why these saints and martyrs carried a stick or staff, and saw themselves eternized with it in frescoes, paintings and statues.

Let us take a closer look at them, as far as we can: Joseph, Jesus' (foster) father is frequently depicted with a staff from which lilies may blossom. St. Macarius and

St. Bathelomew both carry a staff without particular characteristics. St. Dominic supposedly received a staff from St. Peter and St. Paul to accompany him in his preaching pilgrimage through the world. He is said to have rescued drowning pilgrims from the Garonne river, on their way to Santiago de Compostela (1211). Legend has it that this holy cross also saved him and his friends from the pouring rain. And when his books fell into the river, fishermen picked them up three days later, finding them completely dry (Jöckle: 128-9).

We find St.Tranus of Prada and St. Bruno, both represented with a staff lying at their feet. St. Adelbert has a sceptre at his feet. St. Christopher, the unjustly called cynocephalic ogre, became the well-known patron saint of travellers around the globe. He wanted to serve the devil, who was supposed to be mightier than a king. However, when Christopher saw that his master feared the cross, he left him, and started looking for Christ. He devoted himself to carrying pilgrims across a river. There was a small boy he could hardly carry. After the crossing the boy revealed that he was Christ, and predicted that green leaves would sprout from the repentant's staff. Christ himself baptized the repentant ogre and gave him the name of Christophorus (bearer/carrier of Christ). Christopher himself convinced over 8,000 people to receive baptism by showing them his flowering staff. Christopher was eventually either beheaded or drowned in a well (Jöckle: 105-107).

There are St. Martialis, St. Anthony Abbot and St. Raymundus, who used their staff as a mast to sail troubled waters. St. Romuald and St. William of Maleval (?-1157) both carried a T-formed staff. Then there is St. Willibrord, the famous monk from the British Isles who became Bishop of Utrecht in 695. He founded the Dom Cathedral there, and was assigned to Christianize the Low Countries. He baptised numerous heathens in so-called baptismal pools. As a result a large number of pools and wells are associated with this saint. In the Vita it is told that during one of his missionary travels along the coast he was short of drinking water. Legend has it, that after praying fervently, he was able to strike a well with his staff. Its shape and character were unfortunately not documented.

Since the early missionaries frequently choose the *fana* and other sacred heathen places for their preaching. It is hard to say whether Willibrord was really the creator of the wells. The wells could have been associated with him as he Christianized them. In any case, there is evidence that at least a small number of the sacred wells in the Low Countries associated with Willibrord, indeed date back to the time he preached among the Frisians. Therefore these wells became places of pilgrimage[7] (cf. Jöckle: 472-475; Schuyf: 69-71).

We encounter St. Jude, who carried a carpenter's square besides his staff; St. James Minor; St. Fridolin the Pilgrim; St. James the Great, son of Zebedee and brother of John the Evangelist, Jesus's favourite apostle and cousin, unintentionally founder of the pilgrimage to Santiago de Compostela in Spain; St. Judoc, patron saint of pilgrims and seafarers, tamer of birds and fish; St. Roch; St. Pirmin (Pirminus of Reichenau, 724-753), though mostly depicted with a miniature church, an illuminated book, frogs and snakes. Pirinius was able to get rid of all the vermin on the island of Reichenau, and created wells with his staff. Many years later his staff was used to consecrate a well in Luxemburg that had the power to heal children with gland diseases (Jöckle: 372); St. Asaph and Aydan, two local saints from Arles sur Tech in the French Pyrenees, still worshipped (processions are held for them every year); St. Loy, with hammer and staff; St. Philip, the disciple who asked Jesus to show him his father, the saint who planted a stick for the heathens in Hungary, and it immediately flowered. St. Philip is also connected to Walpurgia in Austria; St. Domitian (c. 560) whose iconography shows a dragon at his feet, and a well springing where he put his staff. In Huy (or, Hoey, Belgium) Domitian supposedly killed a dragon that had contaminated a well, and he secured a fresh source for the inhabitants (cf. Brewer, 1870; Heidt, 1955; Jöckle, 2003).

Apart from this multitude of male saints, some female saints as well are represented with a staff: St. Clara (1194-1253), St. Genieve (422-502), St. Gertrude the Great (13th century) and St. Gertrude (626-659) of Nivelles (Nijvel, in Flanders, Belgium), who advocated the advancement of science. She saved the abbey in Nivelles from a blazing fire, and reputedly brought a child that drowned back to life.

The devil represented by mice and rats are crawling up her staff to — unsuccessfully — make her angry and impatient. She is the patron saint of travellers, pilgrims and hospitals.

St. Scholastica, who caused a severe storm when she wept inconsolably after having to say farewell to her brothers; St. Briget (1302/3-1373), and St. Walpurgia (25 February 779) whose name was given to Walpurgis Night — the Night of the Witches at the Eve of May Day, when the evil power of these mischievous creatures was supposed to be at its height. At the same time, however, it was a lucky day for

*St. Jacob*

68

*Crosier*

devout people who washed in the village well to remain young and beautiful (cf. Hiller: 201). Many centuries ago in Bavaria, Tyrol and Bohemia, the ceremony of Burning out the Witches would begin on May Day itself when the bell had rung and twilight was falling (Frazer: 734-5). The saint herself, however, as her legend tells us, calmed a heavy storm at sea by praying (Jöckle: 455).

Remarkably most legends involving saints with a staff as their characteristic object, tell us a tale featuring a key element of human existence: water. According to these stories the staff itself is an instrument enabling the saint to strike a wellspring. Obviously the well itself became a site of worship and eventually even pilgrimage. Either because it had been struck by someone who would later be a saint (the association with the holy person), or thanks to the Christianisation of the sacred source or pool.

There are many other connections with water. A number of 'staffed' saints were able to calm troubled waters, or make rain storms cease with their prayers. St. Dominic and St. Gertrude, for instance, were able to rescue drowning people. St. Dominic has a somewhat special relationship with the element, as the people he saved — they were drowning in the Garonne — were pilgrims on their way to Santiago de Compostela. The dead body of St. James the Great, for whom tens of thousands of pilgrims still walk to Santiago, washed ashore in Gallicia, on Spain's west coast. It was covered with scallop shells.

The staff also served as a mast on ships. It was used as such by various holy characters when they and their companions were almost lost in a storm at sea. Their staff challenged another of the four elements, the air, blowing over restless waters. It is noteworthy that the staff seems to have no different role whether it belongs to a male or a female saint or martyr.

Judging from mythological, historiographical sources, perhaps a large part of all these legends originated from Judeo-Christian mythology, with Moses's rod separating the waters of the Red Sea, allowing his people to cross safely, as we saw earlier.

The staffs of most saints look like those of shepherds. But the origin and evolution of the bishop's, abbot's or abyss's staffs are much more complex, and often not even agreed upon. Male and female saints are often depicted as holding a clerical post.

One might suppose that this is why they carry a staff. However, the stories in which their staffs occur are often much older than their use as a liturgical object. The history of staffs can be traced through well-documented traditions, historiography and apocryphal stories current within the Roman Catholic Church. Its liturgy was and sometimes still is very elaborate. The staff is mostly described as a sign of dignity, jurisdiction and authority. It indicates that its owner, a cardinal or bishop in particular, is holding office. The staff ceased to be a purely pontifical attribute after the tenth or eleventh century. Since that time, the pope has carried the ferula. It has a special significance, based on clerical liturgy.

In any case, in the twelfth century the baculum, as this staff was called, was already acknowledged as an attribute of power and authority: "[...] *Sanctae Romanae Ecclesiae et domini papae Calixti et pro remedo animae meae dimitto Deo et sanctis Dei apostolis Petro et Paulo Sanctaeque Catolicae Ecclesiae omnem investituram per anulum et baculum et concedo in ominibus ecclesis [...]*"

Thus wrote Emperor Henry v to the Pope, when he returned the Church's possessions and proposed peace to Callixtus in Worms in 1122.[8] Indeed, it was such a sign: even today the staff or crosier is entrusted to bishops at their consecration and to mitred abbots at their investiture. On this occasion, the Roman Pontifex expresses the words: "*Accipe baculum pastoralis officii; et sis in corrigendis vitiis pies viens, judicium sine ira tenes, in fovendis virtitubus auditorum animos mulcens, in tranquilitate severitatis censuram non deserens.*"[9]

Legend has it that the end of a staff was sharp and pointed to prick and spur the slothful. The middle part is straight to signify righteous rule, while the top is bent or crooked in order to draw in and attract souls to the ways of God. The crosier acted, and was used as an active sign system for, and by its owner. It was not just a sign of office, it also indicated the rank of the clergy through both qualitative and quantitative indices. Bishops always carry the crosier with the crook turned outwards, while prelates of lower rank hold it with the head reversed. Moreover, an abbot's crosier is not only smaller than that of a bishop, thus having another sign value, it is also covered by a veil when a bishop is present (cf. www. catholicencyclopedia.com), thus obtaining a subordinate character.

Staffs have already been found in catacombs dating back to the fourth century. However a possible liturgical significance cannot be established, despite the fact that Pope Celestine I (d. 432) mentioned it in a letter to the Bishops of Vienne and Narbonne in France. It was as early as the seventh century that the first true reference to the crosier as a liturgical instrument occurred (cf. Heidt: 830; www. catholicencyclopedia.com). The original shape of the crosier was a long stave with a ball or knob at the top (like the makhila!) which survived in Ireland until the twelfth century. Besides, there were early crosiers with a horizontal crook, so-called Tau-staves, used by abbots in particular. They survived until the thirteenth century. Almost entirely throughout the Middle Ages the crosier had a crook bent inwards, frequently shaped like a snake. Leaves appeared under Gothic influence in the fourteenth and fifteenth centuries, and the lower part of the crook was bent outwards. Ever since the crosier became more and more decorated. Originally it more or less looked like a shepherd's staff and it was usually made of cypress wood. Later other materials were used as well, such as metal and ivory.

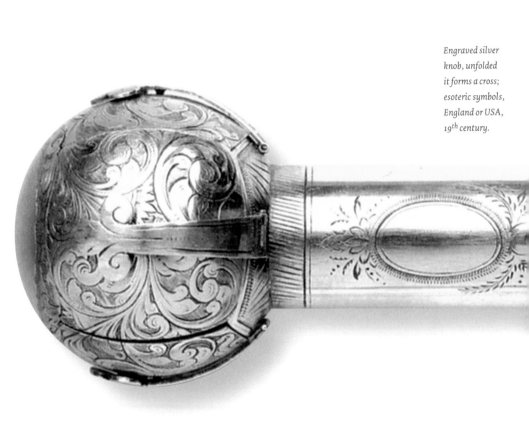

*Engraved silver knob, unfolded it forms a cross; esoteric symbols, England or USA, 19th century.*

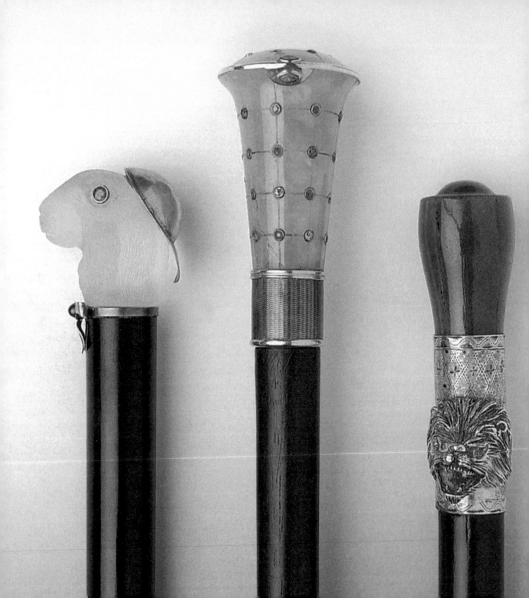

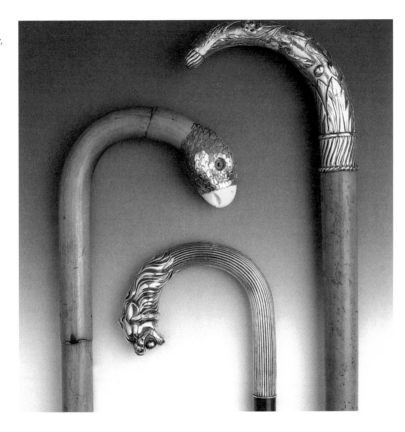

rasc
ver collar,
picture
taly,
ntury.

y.

*Glazed ivory,*
*dotted with silver*
*and tin, England,*
*circa 1700*

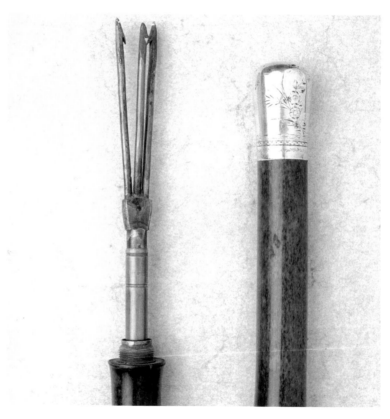

< Poacher
stick, can
a trident
or salmon
end 19th c

Ivory han
mignonet
shaft, Fra
19th centu

Root of th
tree, grot
character
Germany
end 18th c

The staff's origin is often associated with the shepherd's crook. The similarity is obvious. Moreover, the shepherd's flock is associated with the followers of Christ. They should be kept together like sheep and the erring ones should be brought back to the herd. There is also a physical resemblance (iconic relationship) and a ceremonial and liturgical similarity with the lituus,[10] frequently found on Roman coins. The Lituus was a long trumpet of the Etruscan-Roman augurs, shamans of the Classical period. It was the augur's task to determine if a person's future plans would be blessed by the gods.

Thus, the crosier is seen in a completely different light. It is hardly plausible to maintain that it derived from the 'walking-sticks' or staffs used by pilgrims, the so-called bourdons, before there were any seats or benches in chapels and churches (cf. www.catholicencyclopedia.com).

The use of the ferula is restricted to the Pope during the Holy Year,[11] when the Porta Santa (Holy Door) in St. Peter's Cathedral at the Vatican is opened. The ferula is intended to act as a symbol of the Pope's power of governance, which is not limited by place or time, as is the case with the power of bishops and cardinals (Heidt: 290). Though its kinship with the staff is disputed, and its relationship with the sceptre considered more plausible (cf. www.catholicencyclopedia.com; www.new advent.org), both views may be correct. On a conceptual level the ferula is closer to the sceptre as it symbolizes omnipotence. The sceptre does so for the worldly monarch.

Materially, however, the ferula is a descendent of the staff with special features, and a particular symbolic value.

The abacus is the staff of the Templars. It, too, has a cross on top, the Templars' cross. Its medallion form is known as fourchée. It can be found in many chapels and churches in the South of France. In the aftermath of this Order, the Knights of the Templars led a secluded life under threat in castles and villages in deserted areas such as Carcassonne and la Couvertoirade, where the Gnostic Cathars lived as well. Time and again a strong and beguiling connection has been suggested between both groups in popular novels (cf. Brown, 2003) and historiographical research journalism (cf. Lincoln, Leigh & Baigent, 2005 (1982)).

The abacus is a symbol of power, a staff of commandment, which had to be treated with dignity and was not to be touched, except by the Master himself (cf. Marillier). Its obvious significance cannot be described any better than in Sir Walter Scott's Ivanhoe: '*His white mantle was shaped with severe regularity, according to the rule of St. Bernard himself, being composed of what was then called Burrel cloth, exactly fitted to the size of the wearer, and bearing on the left shoulder the octangular cross peculiar to the Order, formed of red cloth. No vair or ermine decked this garment; but in respect of his age, the Grand Master, as permitted by the rules, wore his doublet lined and trimmed with the softest lambskin, dressed with the wool outwards, which was the nearest approach he could regularly made to the use of fur, then the greatest luxury of dress. In*

*Abacus*

*his hand he bore that singular 'abacus', or staff of office, with which the Templars are usually represented, having at the upper end a round plate, on which was engraved the cross of the Order, inscribed with a circle or orle, as heralds term it.'* (Scott, 1819: chap. xxxv n.p. no.).

## The Wand of Wicca

. . . . . . .

The wand is the witch's stick, a very essential attribute that comes with magic spells. It is a symbol of mostly mild supernatural powers, that would or could not be realized or released without it. The traditional wand is mostly a straight hazel

*Wand*

(*Corylus avellena*) stick with the appearance of a cork screw, having either a closed or 'open' spiral. According to modern-day Wicca, young hazel sprouts must be used, having neither blossomed nor born fruit. Witches claim that within original Wicca, a secret knowledge system, virgin hazel was highly valued. The witch is one of the few types of women with a stick among their paraphernalia. It has both a physical and symbolic function. It is used as a means of support. For in folkore and fairy tales the witch is usually 'an old hag'. It also indicates her special powers, particularly when the stick is made of witch hazel. Her benevolent counterpart, the Good Fairy from fairy tales and cartoons, mostly uses a small wand like modern magicians.

The modern conjurer's wand is of a slightly different character. It is a rather small, straight black stick with white tips. It is used as an instrument helping the magician doing his tricks. These tend to be of a much more teasing character than the fairy's magic. She mostly solves problems with it. The magician tinkers with male and female symbols. The cards and dice, the cigarettes and cigars of the masculine are set off against the silk shawls, bunnies and doves representing the feminine (cf. Bouissac, 1976). Runic wands used by proto-historic European tribes also assisted in magic rituals. These wands bore inscriptions and were tossed on a white cloth to be read only by the druids. They based their spells upon the patterns they discovered, and immediately erased (Verhoeven: 16-17). In fact, even the lituus was a sort of wand. As we saw, Roman priests used it when foretelling a person's future.

In the early eighteenth century, so-called running footmen also carried 'wands'. It was these servants job to run ahead or alongside the coaches of the 'great houses' to inform the innkeepers of the arriving guests. They carried a pole to help the cumbrous coach of their master out of numerous sloughs on the highways in Britain. It was called a 'wand,' because it worked wonders for their masters (Brewer: 1084). Nowadays, even notebook computers and electronic agendas (pda's) are operated by means of a small stick called a wand. These electronic devices cannot be operated solely by a keyboard. Frequently, they even lack such a device completely. Touching the sensitive screen with the wand does the trick.

Wands never seem to lose their power, and their magic is as appealing as in the Middle Ages. J.K. Rowling must have used her wand to cast such a spell on billions of people following the feud between Harry Potter and his arch rival Voldemort. The importance of the wand in the Harry Potter books is obvious.

## Material Witnesses

. . . . . .

It is obvious that many species of trees providing natural material for all types of staff, stick or wand, had or still have a special significance stemming from pre- and proto-historic indigenous Germanic and Celtic cosmology. The oak is a well-known example. Court was held under many an oak tree even until the late Middle Ages in North Western Europe (Schuyf: 40-1). Up to the present day, in many places in Europe, pieces of material from the clothes, so-called ex-votos, of ill people are tied to branches of oak or lime trees, begging a saint or the Holy Virgin for healing (Schuyf: 89; Fraanje: 243-8). Trees were also supposed to take away fever. Some blood of an ill person was smeared on the bark of the tree in order to 'transfer' the fever to it. In the Dutch province of Drenthe, an ill person would cast a magic spell on a branch of a hazel tree. If a knob emerged on that branch, the illness would disappear. Until the early 1800's in other areas in The Netherlands a garter was tied

*Ash
(Fraxinus
excelsior)*

around the branch of a tree. The garter had a short rhyme (in the regional dialect) written on it:

> *Olde marolde*
> *Ik hebbe ze noe, ik geve ze oe*
> *Ik bind ze hier neer*
> *Ik krieg ze niet meer*
> (Heuvel in: Schuyf: 89).

> *Old 'marolde' (my old one)*
> *I have it now, I give it to you*
> *I tie it down here*
> *I won't get it no more*

'Kinderbomen' (fertility trees, 'children-trees') existed in popular belief in many places in the Netherlands and elsewhere. The idea remained vivid in the collective memory for many centuries. Even nowadays, trees that people used to say brought them children, can still be found in the centre of rural villages. The same was said of wells and even stones (Schuyf: 89).

Some trees, like the lime tree, were traditionally associated with fertility. Sometimes a young couple would tie a knot in a twig of a tree as a symbol of true, everlasting love. Germanic tribes dedicated the lime tree to Freya, goddess of fertility, love and justice. It was planted at the spot where roaming Germanic tribes settled (Fraanje: 245). Many a lime tree can still be found at market places in villages in The Netherlands and Germany. It is said that Charlemagne promoted planting lime trees in villages, and near houses. Acoording to the old Germanic belief a lime tree protected houses and people against lightning. Right up until historic times, lime trees in front of a house were said to protect it against witches and to cure illnesses (Hiller: 110). There is hardly a tree in the Indo-European traditions with more cultural significance than the lime tree.

Ash (*Fraxinus exelcior*) and alder (*Alnus incana/Alnus glutinosa*) have also been of great importance in European cosmology. They play crucial parts in Germanic mythology, ranging from the ash as the World Tree Yggdrasil, to the Nordic mythical belief that Embla, the first woman, was born from an alder. She was created by the sons of the giant Bôr. Then there was the practice of hiding small twigs under one's pillow during Walpurgis Night to scare off the devil. In the Germanic speaking region the alder is also one of the five prescribed species of deciduous and coniferous trees, from which specific visual signs were (and still are) made for hunters (cf. Frevert, 1936). It has been said that the cross of Jesus was made of alder (Fraanje: 98).

Evidently trees have played a major role in the minds of practically all peoples of ancient Europe. This lasted for centuries, even after the original notions vanished in the mists of time. No wonder that after Christianization original beliefs were regarded as superstitious because they did not comply with the official dogma. However they still influenced ordinary folks, which was disliked by the church.

*Desert Nomads,*
*Fezzan, Libya*
*© Kazuyoshi*
*Nomachi*

One of the most widely used types of wood for making ordinary walking sticks is hazel.[12] Both in Germany and Scotland this tree seems to grow in abundance given the number of walking sticks made there. Hazel has always been part of the millennium old hedgerows in the British Isles (cf. Hoskins, 1967). If these are regularly cared for, they produce fine straight hazel wood sticks. Nowadays, these are very much sought after by an increasing number of walking stick enthusiasts. In tourist regions one will find hazel walking sticks on every street corner. These sticks are generally straight, bearing a naturally grown knob at the thickest end, a leather strap, and a sharp metal tip at the lower end. Most hazel walking sticks are made in one piece. Sometimes they are fitted with a V-formed handle made out of deer antler. These are the more elaborate and expensive models, particularly used by hunters, for reasons we will turn to later.

Hazel has been widely used since prehistoric times. It played an important part in the culture of the ancient Germanic tribes. Hazel nuts and sticks are found as burial gifts in their graves. It had cosmological qualities: hazel was dedicated to Thor or Donor whose lightning bolts looked like hazel branches. These branches, however, were also credited with opposing powers. Until the present day naturally forked hazel twigs[13] are used to find subterranean water or minerals (cf. also Brewer: 360; Hiller: 73-4). After Christianisation, the church was strongly opposed to the use of dowsing rods, and sometimes excluded practitioners of the forked hazel from communion.

The hazel and its nuts have also had a strong association with fertility. Around newly sown land, small hazel sticks used to be put in the ground to get a good crop. This was founded on the Germanic belief that Iduna, the goddess of fertility, was turned into a hazelnut to be liberated later by Loki. A bumper harvest was thought to predict an increase in the number of marriages that year (cf. Brewer: 644; Hiller: 74).

Witch hazel — a species with intricately curled branches like some willows (*Salix alba*) — does not belong to the group of true hazels. But in ancient times it was supposed to have many magic powers. Its forked twigs were used for divining rods, and the name 'witch hazel' originates from this use in folklore (Schuyf: 41). It was, however, also used to locate witches (Brewer: 1307).

Twigs of hazel brought strength and health, and were seen as an excellent protection against snakes. Dangerous animals were easily conquered with a hazel stick. Any foe could be defeated using a stick made of hazel wood, provided it had been cut on Good Friday with three good, clean cuts in the name of the Holy Trinity. Beating the clothes of a person with it, would make him feel the pain wherever he was (cf. Fraanje: 172; Schuyf: 81-89).

The use of antler (in French *le bois*, the wood) for the forked staff handle is not just a coincidence or based on functional reasons alone. Antler is a very special material. Here it acts as a mediator between different domains. It has a very strong vegetative connotation because of the terminology used to describe this part of

*Nenet tribe,*
*March 4, 1993,*
*Antipajuta, Siberia*
© *Jacques Langevin*

a deer's body. It falls off each year, like a dead branch from a tree. Antler also has mythical qualities. It is the ideal material for the hunter's trophy as it can only be procured by killing the male deer or finding its antlers in the field or forest, which is virtually impossible. The deer itself, however, is able to shed off his own trophy, his 'token of victory'. The thrown-off antlers and the hunter's trophy imply a dualistic relationship with death. That is why Christ Himself was represented by the deer in the legends of St. Eustace and St. Hubert. Christ too had this dualistic relationship with death, symbolized by the cross on which he died more or less voluntarily, and left behind by his resurrection (cf. Van den Broek, 1986). How could a hunter be playing more dualistically with life and death than by supporting his gun with a deer's forked antler on a hazel stick, and aiming to shoot exactly such an animal?! Hazel is a symbol of life, because of its special connection with water. Its emblematic qualities, combined with the dualistic symbol of Christ, representing eternal life through his resurrection, forms an ideal relationship of metonymical qualities for the hunter when he decides whether the deer will live or die.

It is clear that choosing hazel for a walking stick or staff was based on persuasive cognitive fundamentals, deeply rooted in Indo-European cosmology, to be Christianised later. A hazel stick proved to be the ideal companion for pilgrims, and all foot travellers because of its alleged powerful and protective qualities. Yet other means were used as well. For instance, to protect them against fatigue hikers would pick some Saint Johnsworth (*Hypericum perforatum*) leaves before dawn, and put them in their shoes. Some garlic in one pocket made walking even more comfortable (cf. Hiller: 97).

Apart from the ascribed qualities, hazel was strongly connected with hidden earth treasures, like water. In Roman Britain hazel was associated with Neptune, the best known water god (Green: 73). In Celtic times, hazel was already strongly associated with water. A number of 'bog people' who were ritually murdered were strangled with rope twined from hazel twigs (Green: 80-1). Because of its strong relationship with water, countless wells were found and struck using hazel wood dowsing rods and staffs. Ancient Irish folklore tells us about nine hazel trees standing near a well at the bottom of the sea.

The type of wood of the staffs of most saints cannot possibly be identified a posteriori. However, many legends featuring the staff of a particular saint as a mast, a tool to divide sea waters or strike a well, all plead for hazel. There seems to be a consistent connection between hazel and the cool liquid element. Hazel has always been sought after for water-related equipment. The fishing-rod for instance, was traditionally made of hazel (cf. Ketting in Walton: 27; Berners, 1496).

Because of its positive and protective qualities as an aid for wanderers, hazel wood was a preferred material for manufacturing walking sticks. It had supernatural, and sometimes secret qualities appropriate for god's lightning bolts, and for

*Macuxi In▮*
*with rapos▮*
*cane, Apri▮*
*Roraima, ▮*
*© Antonio▮*

the runic writing of the druids.[14] In England, in a ritual shaft or pit, dozens of pots have been found wrapped in hazel wood leafs and filled with hazel nuts (Green: 109).

The ash (*Fraxinus,* varies species) must also have been an important provider of material for sticks, staves, staffs and walking sticks. Not just because of the eminent qualities of this wood, but also because of the ancient cognitive characteristics ascribed to it. For the ash was the representation of Yggdrasil, the World Tree, Tree of Knowledge, Tree of Life. It is even the Tree of Time and Space, representing the Blue Heavens and the Green Earth (cf. Van den Broek, 1989: 456-468; Brewer: 1319; Fraanje: 111). The ash was one of the most important trees, and played a major part in Germanic and Nordic mythology. Man was created from an ash, woman from an alder. A similar attribution was found in ancient Greece. In Europe and England, the ash protected against snakes and the witchcraft of trolls, imps and evil spirits (Fraanje: 111-112).

Ash provided numerous ancient cultures with wood for weapons, spears, lances, and bows. The Greek word 'melia', for instance, means 'ash' and 'lance.' Nemesis, the goddess of Revenge, even carried a staff made of it.

The staffs carried on Palm Sunday, celebrating Christ's famous entry of Jerusalem, were made of juniper (*Juniperus communis*), hazel or willow, thus symbolizing fertility and the coming of spring (Hiller: 147). The juniper or palm tree is believed to have sprung from residue of the clay that formed Adam. Hence it is a symbol of resolution overcoming calamity (Brewer: 934). There is an entire array of attributions, and special powers connected with juniper in the folk tales of North-West Europe. Also, there is an equally vast number of names[15] for this mysterious tree. Like many coniferous trees the juniper is an important symbol of eternal life, either because of its essential oils and berries, or thanks to its ever green branches. Like the hazel and the yew (*Taxus baccata*), it provided Germanic tribes with sticks to be decorated with runes. It also played an important part in protecting the homestead against evil powers. Farmers smoked pipes made of juniper wood to protect themselves against evil spirits (cf. Fraanje: 203). Later, it was found in the St. Mary-cult in Europe. A juniper allegedly provided shelter for Mary, Joseph, and Jesus when they were escaping from Herod's soldiers. Folklore has many connections to the supernatural, whether Christian or pagan. The choice to use juniper for the staff carried by children on Palm Sunday must be culturally and cognitively determined, and not functionally. The connotation of eternal life for these objects used at Easter is, of course, too obvious to conclude otherwise.

The makhila is made of the medlar tree, not only because of the wood quality. In the Low Countries not just the wood, but also the fruit of the medlar was highly appreciated for its wholesome qualities. It offered people protection against illness because of its high level of vitamin C, though it had probably not been recognized pharmaceutically. In Flanders the medlar was popularly called 'a little support in wintertime.'

In a figurative way the 'staff' is related to bread as the most common food in many parts of the world. It provides a larger share of people's energy and protein than any other food. Bread is often called the 'staff of life,' alluding to a staff supporting the feeble in walking (Brewer: 1172).

It is clear that the choice of wood for a cane, stick, baton or staff has always been based on cultural and attributed values and significance, rather than on functional qualities. Though many trees had supernatural powers in the minds of our distant ancestors, only a few were considered suitable to be used for walking sticks or staffs. The materials used to produce artefacts may serve as tangible evidence for cognitive domains. Moreover, the cognitive value of particular materials, such as types of wood from specific species of trees, enables man to mediate between different cognitive domains that would be hard to converge otherwise (cf. Van den Broek, 1991, 2006). As we have seen, one of the most convincing examples of this is hazel, because of its ascribed quality of protecting the bearer of a hazel stick. This had to do with Thor/Donar, the upper gods of ancient European religions, who used lightning as a sign of ultimate power. Lightning and water are opposing elements attracting each other. Lightning hits water much more frequently than land. At the same time the hazel twig was used to find hidden treasures such as water, thus mirroring the contrariety in mythology and nature itself. A Holy man striking a well with a hazel staff parallels Thor/Donar's lightning bolt hitting the water. They are each other's metaphor.

## Signs of Descent / Signs of Arrival

. . . . . . .

The cane was, and sometimes still is, also used as a vehicle for *aides mémoires* elements: little shields may still be bought at touristic places. They are nailed on the stick to indicate where it had been, to show off to fellow hikers. This tradition is kept alive mostly in Germany, though these mostly iconic symbols form the self-attained award for a hiking tour in The Netherlands as well. After a while the itinerary of a hiker may very well be reconstructed following the trail of the successive order of the souvenir shields.

These shields, badges or insignia leave the impression that they have a heraldic character, and indeed they have. The use of insignia in Europe probably started in 1097, when the Crusaders besieging Antioch used shield symbols for their identification. Later nobility adopted insignia as family coats of arms, and orders of knighthood. These emblems (and not just symbols, cf. Van den Broek, 1991) included heavily jewelled necklaces and medals, and other extravagant ornaments. The first real coat

*Escutcheon and Apoth*

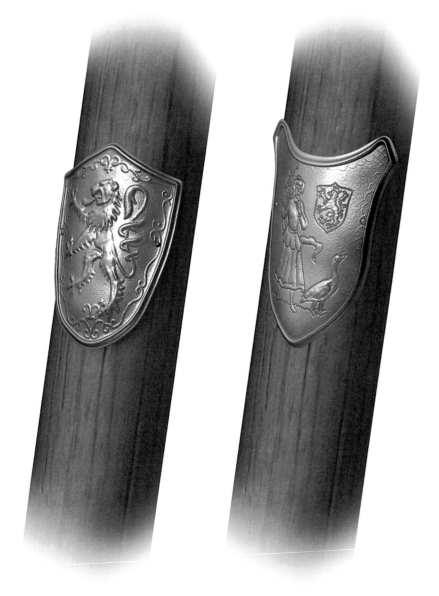

of arms appeared during the early 1100's among crusaders wearing heavy armour during battle. Because the helmets fully covered their faces they started to show coats of arms on their shields and flags so to be recognized on the battlefield.

Heraldry also served as a means of identification in civilian life. In the Middle Ages landowners gave other nobles the use but not the ownership of land in exchange for their military and other services, where the stick acted as a pars pro toto. Members of the upper classes, royalty, nobility and clergy identified their possessions and official documents by marking them with their coats of arms.

By the 1200's heraldry was institutionalized as a system of identification. Upper-class families passed their coat of arms down from one generation to the next. By custom, and eventually by heraldic law, no two families could use the same coat of arms. The many heraldic designs and possible confusion among them led to the formation of a group of men regulating these matters. This class consisted of officials called heralds. Originally heralds were mere messengers carrying missives to and fro the knights and their armies. They announced and directed tournaments, and conducted certain ceremonies. The heralds had to know one knight from another to perform their duties. Heraldic symbols provided the necessary identification.

The duties and responsibilities of the heralds increased as heraldry expanded and involved more and more families. Finally heralds became responsible for

*hild (left)*
*cium*

keeping track of families and their coat of arms. In addition they created the so-called armorials in which the heraldic designs were recorded. They also developed a jargon known as blazonry to describe the arms. The right and left (dexter and sinister)[16] were mirrored and the names of the various colours differed significantly from the ordinary terminology. There are two basic forms for a coat of arms: the escutcheon, or triangular shaped , and apothecium, a more complex form. They mostly bear the name and an object from the particular region that stands for this area. As such it is a chosen sign, acting as a symbol for it.

## Commoners' Heraldy

. . . . . .

The pilgrim's staff is very similar to the traditional and modern cane in the sense that both indicate a challenge the moment they are in the hands of the traveller. They are the vehicles for their signs of victory. Pilgrimage has a modern day equivalent. For both hiker and pilgrim the tour is a goal in itself. At the same time reaching one's destination is the climax of religious or quasi-religious experiences. A serious hiking tour is the modern day pilgrimage. Both imply a strenuous, sometimes even hazardous journey on foot with a highly significant destination, be it a natural or a religious symbol. Many long distance hikers have even adopted the essential accessories used by medieval pilgrims: the pera, typical bag borrowed from Egyptian monks, and containing all the necessary paperwork for pilgrims (a letter of recommendation, a letter of faith and communion), baculum (staff, which served to show the owner's devotion), and ligula (sandals), the ever present hat,[17] cape, and even St. Jacob's shell (used to drink water).

Although most long distance pilgrim's routes were, and still are to be found all over Europe, this — lay — tradition is still particularly alive in the German-speaking countries. In every tourist village and at every tourist site a variety of 'insignia' can be bought for just a handful of change. The basic form is mostly that of the escutcheon. Printed over it is the name of a particular tourist attraction, or the city or village where it is located. One model of souvenir proves to fit numerous different places. At these sites, however, other models may be obtained too: bas relief impressions of European wild turkey, or a red deer's head with antlers, with a small escutcheon shield and the name of the site underneath. These insignia can also be found in numerous tourist places, and only the name indicates where they are from. Such a tiny shield on a walking stick has an emblematic meaning. The contrast with a heraldic sign is that it does not indicate where one is from, or rather whom the shield represents, but where one has travelled, which place was reached. It almost seems a trophy, $\tau\rho o\pi\alpha\iota o\nu$ (tropaion), 'sign of victory.'

Pilgrims' insignia were mostly bought at the spot, and nailed to the baculum. Frequently they took the form of small ceramic tiles, or pictures of the visited place, shells or copies of relics. In the Middle Ages in some villages and cities along the famous pilgrims' routes (such as Rocamadour in South-West France) an entire industry emerged. The tiny shields did not just testify that the pilgrim actually visited the holy places, but were also meant as memorative signs. The real evidence was a certificate signed by a high official of the clergy (cf. Mous: 52-53). Moreover, a successful pilgrimage resulted in the absolution of all sins one had committed during his life. Apart from pilgrims carrying their baculum, there were 'palmers'. These privileged pilgrims carried a consecrated palm-staff. Unlike the ordinary pilgrim, the palmer spent his entire life visiting shrines, particularly in the Holy Land, while living off charity (Brewer: 935). The following rhyme is by Sir Walter Scott:

> His sandals were with travel tore
> Staff, budget, bottle scrip he wore
> The faded palm-branch in his hand
> Showed a pilgrim from the Holy Land.
> (Marmion, i. 27)

The pilgrims highly valued relics, much more valuable items compared to the common insignia. The urge to take something home from the holy places became so great that a vivid trade in relics emerged as early as the fourth century, right after Emperor Constantine made Christianity the official religion in his realm. Constantine's mother identified the first holy places: the Cave of Nativity in Bethlehem, the place of the Ascension on the Mount of Olives, and the Holy Sepulchre in Jerusalem. Thus pilgrimage to the burial places of saints and the places where Jesus had walked became institutionalised (cf. Feinberg Vomosh, 2000; Heidt: 405-411). Jerusalem, Rome and Santiago de Compostela became the most famous and visited places of pilgrimage.[18]

Centuries later, this 'little tradition' was taken over by motorists, putting self-adhesive emblems on the windows of their cars and caravans, thus indicating the usually foreign places they visited. Canes and cars can easily bear a dozen of suchs signs. The habit it seems is nowadays usually considered to be lower middle, and lower class. Nevertheless every souvenir shop in Europe sells them, and caravans still seem to be the most suitable place to put them. The seasoned traveller is known by the signs of the places he has visited. A mere sticker showing a moose on a car or caravan is a clear indication that the vehicle has been to Sweden. This non-verbal, iconic sign clearly stands for the challenge one has met. Sweden, just as the North Cape in Norway and the Polar Circle, is more or less regarded as 'the last frontier' of tourism. Vast forests and barren grounds can still be conquered in these Scandinavian countries. At least, that is what conventional wisdom in Europe takes it for. The 'moose'[19] is a sign of such a victory, a trophy, for everyone to see and admire.

## The Eternal Stick

. . . . . . .

The branch has come a long way and it still has a bright future. It is obvious that the stick has a long and complex genealogy, and that all members of this extended family function as sign vehicles, each in their own way. Resourceful as we are, we find a specific task for the stick as soon as we need one.

It is significant that four out of the five domains in which the representatives of the stick and the club play a key role, have a highly collective, ritual character. Be it the martial, the liturgical, the ceremonial and even the recreational, every one of these domains is controlled by prescribed rules and regulations. All the action taking place is known beforehand and the outcome is certain, even in battle or in a game: one wins, one loses, or it is a draw. It is significant to be able to observe that the descendants of the stick have much more 'peace-loving' members than the descendants of the club, especially when these play an official role. Compare the crosier with the sceptre as attributes of the clergy and the king, respectively. The 'ordinary' walking stick has an individualistic ritual character. Yet it still has an obviously symbolic, cultural significance. It, too, acted or acts as a sign vehicle, telling passers-by one's profession, one's wealth, or even one's handicap.

The stick, staff or wand is an object of material culture that has the ability to carry a multitude of overt and covert messages. It may unite and separate social classes or converge them while they are so different at the same time. In the nineteenth century, the bourgeoisie as well as riff-raff used the cane as a sign for their own class (cf. Veblen, 1899). The cane is either a sign of leisure or a weapon. The stick or the club is nearly always a symbol of power, in whatever disguise it presents itself. Ranging from the conductor's baton to the bishop's crosier, people are governed or guided, find water or punish their fellow man with it. The stick is predominantly a male artefact. Formerly, a woman using a stick in a Western city, for example, surely must have been handicapped. On the other hand, a man with a walking stick might very well be considered a flamboyant personality.

The stick has the power to heal or hurt, to divide and conquer. It is the attribute of the saint and the villain, the magician and the fairy, to play tricks and to deceive. It is a symbol of omnipotence as in the case of the sceptre. The stick or the staff is a companion or a sign of dignity. At the same time it might be a sneaky place to hide a dagger or gun.

The basic material for the stick or staff seems consciously chosen, and based on ascribed inherent qualities of the tree providing the wood. It is obvious that the choice of wood to make a cane, stick, baton or staff must have been deliberate. Not so much because of functional qualities, but mostly on the basis of attributed values and significance. Although there are many species of trees that had supernatural powers in the minds of our ancestors, only a few were considered suitable for making walking sticks and staffs. The material used for making artefacts may serve as tangible evidence for cognitive domains, worlds of thought. The symbolic significance of the various trees that supplied the wood connects one cultural or cognitive domain with another, enabling participants from a culture to cross over. As a result, otherwise possibly insurmountable gaps may be closed (cf. Van den Broek, 1991, 2006). The choice of material for making a stick, staff or sceptre gives this object of material culture another, almost emblematic significance, thus doubling its power. And power they have. All members of the pedigree of the branch, the stick and the club. They can execute physical power by their sheer characteristics and purpose, or symbolic power over millions if they stand for imperial omnipotence.

Nowadays we may notice a comeback of the stick. For instance as a piece of high tech carbon fibre equipment in Nordic walking. The powerful wand of Harry Potter and Gandalf's staff are seen on the silver screen. The cane returns, it seems to be eternal. In the future our offspring will experience exactly the same power of the stick as our ancestors must have felt the moment they first held a cane.

1   I owe this notion in particular to the anthropologist, proto-semiotician and etho-cinematographer Prof. dr. Adrian A. Gerbrands (1917-1997).

2   It is remarkable, to say the least, that due to a serious birth defect, Tut Ankh Amun, who ruled in Thebes as Pharaoh, limped and had to use a cane; several were found in his tomb, according to a recent 'Discovery' television documentary.

3   My own observations were confirmed by the small brochure to be obtained at the castle of Beaufort, Luxembourg.

4   Athena herself is depicted with a staff in a bas-relief on a tomb from c. 450 BC. She was the ruler of the spiritual and moral side of life (Hope Moncrieff: 13).

5   James Smith and Sons, at Hazelwood (!) House still exists today, at 53 New Oxford Street, London.

6   By producing the famous Viennese coffee-house chair No. 14, Thonet introduced the first class-less piece of furniture available to anyone. In the thirties of the twentieth century Thonet extends his product line with steel, chrome pipe furniture; designs from Mart Stam, Marcel Breuer, and Mies van der Rohe, who were closely connected to the Bauhaus group. This family enterprise is now being led by its fifth generation of Thonet, and is in its 180th year. So, it would be ungrateful to give Thonet only the credit for the curved walking stick; his invention led to millions of sturdy, natural and at the same time elegant chairs, tables, and other small household furniture to be found in the Four Corners of the world.

7   Wells formed a significant natural element in the Celtic cosmology. In large areas in Europe new wells were and are honoured together with the saint who is said to have struck it (Schuyf: 42).

8   Concordat passed at Worms between Pope Callixtus II and Emperor Henry V, on September 23, 1122, written by Frederic, Archbishop of Cologne and Recognised Arch Chancellor; Bibliotheca Apostolica Vatican, parchment. The anulum (ring) and baculum (staff) are being recognized and acknowledged here as the distinguishing paraphernalia of the Pope, indicating his papal power - implying that only the scepter is the Emperor's symbol of (worldly) power.

9   'Take this official pastoral staff; correct vices, stimulate piety, administer punishment and thus rule and govern with a gentleness that is tempered with severity.'

10  The name 'lituus' was also used for the cavalry trumpet of the Romans, which, like the wand of the Augurs was crooked with a length of four to five feet, a narrow bore and ending in a conical bell joint turned up in such a manner as to give

the instrument the shape of the letter 'J'.

11  Year wherein the faithful are bestowed with special favours, dating from around 1300; it is held every 50, 33 and 25 years (cf. Heidt, 1955).

12  Haesel in Anglo-Saxon is hat or cap, the cap nut, 'the nut enclosed in a cap' (cf. Brewer: 589). Even in Greek, the hazelnut is referred to as 'the helmet,' korus (cf. Thoreau, 2000: 160), which is more plausible than the supposed meaning (Fraanje, 1999) of the Anglo-Saxon 'haes' to 'command'.

13  'Twig' comes from the Old English and Frisian twâ, two.

14  The Goths are presumed to have been the inventors of the runic script. The handwriting of the gothic Bible of bishop Ulfilas (fourth century) is based on runic characters.

15  In (ancient) Dutch dialect, i.e.: wakel, wachte, aposteemkruid, bekelboom, dambeer, pekke, nijvelboom, krammetboom, machandel, lambeeren palmboom (Fraanje: 201).

16  In blazonry, the dexter (from the Italian destra = right hand side) of a shield as seen from the wearer's viewpoint is the right hand side, and the sinister (from the Italian sinistra), the left-hand side.

17  In England a pilgrim's hat was called a cockle hat. As the chief places of worship were beyond the sea or on the coast, pilgrims used to put cockleshells upon their hats to indicate they were pilgrims (Brewer: 270). Probably it was just because in England there are hardly Jacob scallops to be found, the sign of the pilgrim going to Santiago de Compostela. This particular shell became the symbol for St. James the Great (beheaded in Jerusalem in 44 AD, under Herodus Agrippa), because of the fact that his body was covered with these after it was thrown into the sea off the coast in Galicia (Spain) and brought ashore around 825 (cf. Jöckle: 228-30).

18  Other famous places of pilgrimage in the West are Walshingham and Canterbury in England; Fouvières, Puy, St. Denis, and Lourdes in France; Loretto, Genetsano and Assisi in Italy; Guadelupe and Montserrat in Spain; Ötting, Zell, Cologne, Trier and Einsiedeln in Germany, and dozens more lesser known places of worship and pilgrimage, also in Belgium and The Netherlands (cf. Brewer: 979).

19  It is remarkable, probably because of its inherent emblemetic qualities, that one of the last words uttered by Henry D. Thoreau, the proto-ecologist (1818 - 1862), was 'moose' (cf. Van Doren Stern, 1970).

Amberger, J. Christoph — *The Secret History of the Sword; Adventures in Ancient Martial Arts.* 1998, Multi-Media Books, Burbank, USA, www.ankhonline.com/sceptres.htm

Atkin, Ross — *A Collapsed History of the Umbrella*, 2004, on: The Home Forum, www.csmonito.com

Baigent, Michael, Richard Leigh and Henry Lincoln — *Holy Blood, Holy Grail; the Secret History of Jesus, the Shocking Legacy of the Grail.* 2005 (1982), Delacorte Press, New York

Barret/Gurgand — *Ils voyageaient La France. Vie et traditions des compagnons du tours de France au 19ème siècle.* 1974, Hachette, Paris

Barrte, G. — *Ils voyagaient la France; vie et traditions des compagnons du tour de France.* 1980, Hachette, Paris

Bellis, Mary — *Umbrella.* 2004, on: http://inventors.about.com/library/inventors/blumbrella.htm

Berners, Dame Julia (Barners)—1496 A Treatyse of Fyshhynge with an Angle, in: *The Book of Saint Albans*, Imprinted at London in Fleetestreate at the Sygne of the Rose Garlande, by Wylliam Coplande for Rychard Tottell

Biel, Timothy L. — *The Age of Feudalism.* 1994, Lucent Books, San Diego, CA., USA

Bloch, Marc — *Feudal Society.* 1964 (1961), Univ. of Chicago Press (Reprint), Chicago

Bouissac, Paul — *Circus and Culture; a Semiotic Approach.* 1976, Indiana University Press, Bloomington, IN., USA

Boxma, Willem — De goastok, van traditie tot souvenier. in: *Traditie*, 6/3, 2001

Brewer, E. Cobham — *The Dictionary of Phrase and Fable.* 1870 (1979), Avanel Books, New York

www.cannes-fayet.com

www.catholicencyclopedia.com

Clarke Nuttall, G. — *Trees and How They Grow.* 1916, [s.i.] Cassell

Confédération Compagnonnages Européen/ Europaïsche Gesellenzünfte, on:www.rolandsbruderwk.de

Egberts, Thelma — Markelose 'goastok' weer in trek. in: *Landleven*, 9/5, 2004

Feinberg Vomosh, Miriam — Pilgrims and Profits. in: *Eretz Weekly*, January 2000

Fraanje, Peter J. — *Natuurlijk bouwen met hout; 33 boomsoorten die zich thuisvoelen in Nederland.* 1999, Uitgeverij Jan van Arkel: Utrecht

Frazer, Sir James — *The Golden Bough; A Study in Comparative Religion.* (abbr. ed.) 1890 (1991)

Frevert, Walter — *Das Jagdliche Brauchtum.* 1936 (1981), Paul Parey, Hamburg, Berlin

Gardiner, A. — *Egyptian Grammar.* 1976, Grifith Institute, Oxford

www.gemeinde-gersdorf.de

Green, Miranda J. — *Exploring the World of the Druids* (transl. into Dutch by Catalien and Willem van Paasen). 1997 (2002), Atrium/Icob, Alphen a/d Rijn

Heidt, A.M. (ed,) — *Catholica, geïllustreerd encyclopedisch vademecum voor het Katholieke leven.* 1955, N.V. Uitgeversmaatschappij Pax, 's-Gravenhage

Hiller, Helmut — *Atlas van het bijgeloof.* 1986 (1987), Bosch & Keuning NV, Baarn

Hilton, Rodney H. — *English and French Towns in Feudal Society.* 1992, Cambridge University Press, Cambridge

Hope Moncrieff, A.R. — (sic) *Classic Myth and Legend* (transl.: Klassieke mythologie). 1992, Rebo Reproductions, Lisse

Hoskins, W.G. — *Fieldwork in Local History.* 1967, Faber & Faber, London

Jöckle, Clemens — *Lexikon der Heiligen* (transl.: Heiligen van alle tijden). 2003, Verba, Hoevelaken

Lam, Aboubracry Moussa — *Batôns, massues et sceptres d'Égypte ancienne et d'Afrique noire.* 2003

Lamberti, Alfredo — *Bastoni da passeggio/Walking sticks.* 1994, Itinerari d'Immagini, Magnum, Milano

Marillier, Bernard — n.d. *Essai sur la symbolique Templiere.* Editions Prades, Paris

Mauss, Marcel — *Essai sur le don* (transl.: The Gift; forms and functions of exchange in archaic society). 1925 (1974), Routlegde & Kegan Paul, London

Mous, Huub — *Pylgers nei Fryslân, De Friese pelgrimage.* 2000, Stichting Frysk Festifal, Leeuwarden

Neubecker, Ottfried — *Elzeviers gids van de heraldiek.* 1981 (1979), Elzevier, Amsterdam, Bruxelles (A Guide to Heraldry, transl. by Jhr. R.C.C. de Savorin-Lohman)

www.newadvent.org

Poly, Jean-Pierre, and Eric Bournazel — *The Feudal Transformation.* 1990, Holmes & Meier, Teaneck, NJ., USA

Reaske, Christoppher R. — *Croquet, The Gentle but Wicket Game.* 1988, E.P. Dutton, New York

www.rechtschaffene-zimmerer.de

Scott, Sir Walter — *Marmio, a tale of Flodden Field.* 1808, Constable, Edinburgh

*Ivanhoe, a Romance.* 1819 [1987], Oxford University Press, Oxford

Schlüter, Dick — *Met den koorde of door het zwaard. Criminele rechtspraak, dood- en lijfstraffen in Twente vanaf de middeleeuwen.* 1994, Twents-Gelderse Uitgeverij De Bruijn, Oldenzaal

Segas, M.G.W. — *Brèves histoires de cannes.* 2002, on: www.canesegas.com

Schuyf, Judith — *Heidens Nederland, zichtbare overblijfselen van een niet-christelijk verleden.* 1995, Matrijs, Utrecht

120

www.sticks.org — *Development and History of English Walking sticks*. 2000

Thoreau, Herny D. — *Wild Fruits*. Bradley P. Dean (ed.). 1850-1859 (2000), W.W. Norton & Company, New York, London

Van den Broek, Gerard J. — Signs of Manipulation; Trout, Saint and the Divine Stag. In: *The Nature of Culture*, Walter Koch (ed.), 1986, Brockmeyer, Bochum

Totemismus in der Industriekultur; Markenzeichen in der Volksrepublik China. In: *Zeitschrift für Semiotik*, 1991, Bnd. 13, Heft 1-2

Traps for Fish, Nets for Birds. The Evolution of Semantic Domains. In: *Kultur Evolution, Fall studien und Synthese*, Marlene Landsch, Heiko Karnowski, Ivan Bistrina (eds.), Peter Lang. 1992, Frankfurt a/M, Berlin, Bern, New York, Paris, Wien

The Tangible Mediator; Solid Evidence for Cognitive Domains. In: *Man Signs Nature*, in print, 2005

Van Doren Stern, Philip — *The Annotated Walden*. 1970, Bramhall House, New York

Van Lennep, Jacob — *Ferdinand Huyck*, 1840

Van Os, P. — Lemma on Hobbes. In: *Geschiedenis-kalender*, 2001, SDU Uitgevers, Den Haag

Veblen, Thorstein — *The Theory of the Leisure Class*. 1899, MacMillan Company, New York

Verhoeven, Cornelis — *De mythe van het schrijvers-schap*. 1980, Bzztôh, Den Haag

Walton, Sir Izaac — *The Compleat Angler, or the Contemplative Man's Recreation*. 1653 (1974), Rich. Marriot, London (transl. by Kees Ketting, A.J.G. Strengholt: Naarden)